my heart

EVERY BEAT
SURRENDERED
TO OUR
UNCHANGING GOD

JULIE MANNING

B&H
PUBLISHING GROUP

NASHVILLE, TENNESSEE

978-1-4336-4404-7

Published by B&H Publishing Group
Nashville, Tennessee

Dewey Decimal Classification: 234.2
Subject Heading: HEART—DISEASE \ FAITH \ HOPE

1 2 3 4 5 6 7 8 • 21 20 19 18 17

Contents

Foreword

My physical heart works just fine as far as I know, but my emotional heart–my soul–is a little more touch and go.

Over the course of my life I've been blessed to have many friends who bring different, valuable, and needed gifts to my life. Some who make me laugh till I cry and some who help me know what "not to wear." Some who are present when something tragic hits our lives and you don't know what to do and some who help me parent better. Then there is Julie Manning. Julie gets an entire category. She brings transcendence to my life that causes me to ache for heaven and live less afraid of the worst that may hit me on Earth.

The last few years have brought some difficulties for my family and me. And as is common, in the valleys of our lives, with the sun barely peeking over the mountain crests far above, you start to doubt Jesus, you start to wonder if He sees you, if He has forgotten you, if He is good?

Julie has walked through those valleys right beside me. Despite her own brushes with death and other unique circumstances, she's walked right beside me and continually whispered in my ear, "Yes, Jesus sees you, no He has not forgotten you, yes He is good." And when someone who lives with the ever-present realization that life could end at any given moment speaks those words, they mean an awful lot. Cliché trite statements aren't possible when you know the fragility of life here, the way that Julie does.

There is another gift Julie gives me and will give you too. She knows down to her marrow that sheer presence with Jesus is better . . .

Jesus is better than any acquisition on Earth.

Jesus is better than any relationship here.

Jesus is better than any dream coming true.

You'd think the way I am describing her, she might live somber or serious all the time. But if you are blessed to meet Julie in real life, you'll see her curls bouncing as she talks about Jesus, her eyes all lit up, her voice joyful and nearly child-like and full of wonder, full of hope, full of excitement for whatever lay ahead both here and in our home to come.

Julie tells me all the time that I can't cry at her funeral; I have to celebrate because she will be celebrating. And I tell her all the time that she can't go first because she is who I want by my bed if I find myself sick and dying.

So as we race toward heaven together, it brings me the greatest pleasure in the world to introduce you to my daily "life" running friend, Julie Manning.

Her story will change you.

Her joy will amaze you.

And I pray her faith will unleash upon your life as you run beside her for a little while in these pages.

—Jennie Allen, founder of IF:Gathering

Opening Letter to Readers

I do not believe that I am the only woman whose mind wrestles with her soul. I believe others of you also fight against the angst of pride, comfort, control, comparison, and the feeling that your life is insignificant. Only the Lord knows that this book would not have been written had His Holy Spirit not intervened and created such a strong conviction that my introvert self could not ignore. The Lord took this little girl who would much rather be a fly on the wall and sat my busy-bee hiney down in a chair long enough to bare my soul in front of a computer screen. The result of that time is the book you now hold in your hands.

Were there moments of doubt? Absolutely. In fact, I battled through great mountains of doubt, fear, and insecurity. Yet spending time soaking up the Word of God, worshipping Him in song, and praying my heart out would ground my soul in obedience. I have learned much through this process. Possibly the greatest lesson for me has been learning that joy abides through obedience; joy can be experienced even in the hard obedience, calling for something so scary and so vulnerable. I have spent many days bowing my head and asking for increasing faith. I am not a writer by trade. Yet the Lord opened my heart just enough to pen some words and thoughts down on paper. Elisabeth Elliot once said, "Don't dig up with doubt what was planted with faith." Elisabeth, thank you for being brave enough, allowing these words to leave your mouth and land upon my heart decades after they were spoken. Your life and your obedience have been an encouragement in faith to more women than you will ever know. Lord, would You use the following pages to be just a fraction of encouragement to other women in this day and age.

Joy abides through obedience.

Through writing, the Lord has helped me realize some things. Today I was reminded that there is purpose in me sharing my story beyond merely allowing my three boys to know their mommy and the amazing nearness of our miraculous God. By sharing with others the moment where I stared Jesus in the face, I allow my eyes to see God move and watch His hand at work. I also allow my mind and heart to remember what He has done and, thus, fan the flame of faith and hope in my forever home with God.

Another realization I've had through the process of writing is that God's pursuit of my soul has not ended and truthfully will never end. He desires all of me—all of my worship, all of my affection. He is showing me that He is worth more than anything this life can offer—more than the trivial, to the things I somehow value most.

I want you to know this is not just my story. It can be your story, too. It can be a means through which, I pray, you see how Jesus is pursuing after your soul, your worship, and your full affections. And, in return, may He give you the courage to live with vulnerability, urgency, and intentionality as you share your own story . . . your own heart.

Lord, You alone are the God who was, who is, and who is to come. You are unchanging, and Your pursuit after Your children is unending. I ask that You will draw near to every single person that reads the words on these pages. No matter what season of life—whether in the valley, the desert, the mountaintop, or the plateau. I pray that You will show up in their lives with power, with compassion, with love, and with conviction. I pray You will show Yourself worthy of their every affection. I pray that You meet their every need. And I pray You will turn each heart toward worship of the One who gave His all for our behalf. Jesus, give Your children perseverance until the day when our faith becomes sight.

my heart, julie

Chapter 1

A New Beginning

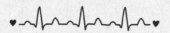

"For the word of the LORD is right,
and all His work is trustworthy."
Psalm 33:4

The rising sun burned brightly that Monday morning. Noah enthusiastically and proudly climbed up into the stroller as I loaded his snack, sippy cup, and a handful of his favorite books to be within reach.

"You ready, buddy?" I asked.

"Yes!" Noah shouted with a grin, and we headed out for our morning walk. It would be our last stroller ride, just the two of us. Noah's life was about to be rocked. Who am I kidding? My life was about to be rocked. Noah's little brother, Hunter, would be born the next morning. Life always seems clearer in hindsight, but for now, as Noah and I hooked a right and climbed the steep hill to exit our street, we simply enjoyed another read through *Green Eggs and Ham.*

At the ripe age of twenty months, Noah had grown comfortable talking about "Baby Brother" as he grew in my belly. Yet the thought of "Baby Brother" actually being born produced a scowl on the toddler's face, almost as if Noah was saying, "Why? Why? Why would we open up a can of worms and let the little guy out?" If only I could share with him the amount of belly-hurting laughter his younger brother would produce in his life. If only I could make a twenty-month-old realize he was about to meet his best friend. If only I could share with him how much his little brother would look up to him and esteem him. If only I could share that the two of them would be inseparable. But for now all I could tell Noah was, "Don't worry, Buddy, I won't let Brother eat your goldfish . . . at least, not for a while."

Sometimes I feel like that twenty-month-old with limited perspective. Looking back, I wish the Lord could have sat me down to tell me all the beautiful things that would bloom through the season I was about to enter. If only I could have seen how He would endure me, breathe life into me, and win my affections, then maybe, just maybe, the next few months and even years would not have been so terrifying as I battled fears and unknowns.

The alarm clock began abruptly buzzing at 5:00 a.m. I had been awake since 4:30, mostly with the anticipation of finally getting to meet the little fighter that had been kicking my rib cage and bladder for the last nine months. As I rolled over to awaken my man, who did not even flinch with the sounding alarm, I gave him a kiss on the cheek and loudly said, "Come on, Baby, it's Go Time!" Yet, in his steadfast and unshaken manner, John somehow convinced me to lie in his arms for five more minutes. And then . . . he quietly started to pray. John prayed for our day, the birth of our son, for Noah, for me, for us. It was just what this anxious mommy needed. I needed to sit still and feel the presence of Jesus.

My mother had graciously come into town the night before to keep Noah. Before tiptoeing out of the house to make the drive to the hospital, John and I snuck into Noah's room. We kissed his sweet little head, and I whispered in his ear, "You are going to meet Hunter today. He loves you already. Mommy loves you. I'll see you soon."

As John and I drove to the hospital, the darkness of the sky was transitioning to a beautiful mix of orange, pink, and red as the sun began to peek itself over the horizon. Hand in hand, we sat in peaceful silence as we watched the beauty of the sunrise. As we were pulling up next to Rudy's BBQ store and gas station, our eyes met, and John gave me one of his smirky little smiles. "No!" I said with a flirtatious hint, "You may not stop to get a breakfast taco, John Manning! We have a baby to meet!" John responded in the most serious of tones, "But that didn't stop me when Noah was born." It is true.

On the morning of Noah's birth, we just "happened" to need gas in the car. John conveniently pulled into Rudy's for gas *and* two breakfast tacos. I still chuckle as I recall the expression on the woman's face at the hospital registration desk as she observed this husband chowing down on his breakfast as he led his laboring wife into the hospital. With a huge grin on his face, he said, "Well, there's no reason why both of us have to go hungry this morning." I shook my head and flirtatiously rolled my eyes, as I laughed at this opening comment. John Manning, my comedian!

However, on this particular morning, John would have to skip the Rudy's taco tradition for no other reason than the kitchen had not yet opened for the day. John loves messing with me, and he thinks it is superhilarious. Key word here is "he" (wink!). Truth be told, I think it's funny too . . . most of the time. I am incredibly thankful for my husband. Not only does he lead our family well, but he makes us all laugh as he leads.

As John and I arrived at the hospital, we followed the arrows affixed to the cream-colored walls with the hope that one of the arrows would land us at the labor and delivery unit. When we began to see canvas prints of infant faces hanging decoratively throughout one particular hallway, we knew we were in the right place. We introduced ourselves to the women behind the registration desk, and as soon as our names exited our mouths, we were whisked away to the preoperative area. I double-checked the clock on the wall and thought, *We aren't late, are we?*

Hunter, like Noah, would be born via a planned cesarean section. I was provided a hospital gown and a pair of those way-too-big hospital socks with the nonslip grippers on both sides. Then the nurse motioned in the direction of the bathroom and said, "Go ahead and empty your bladder while you are in there changing, Honey." I barely had enough time to find a comfortable position on the hospital bed when I heard my ob-gyn's voice as he entered the room.

In typical jovial fashion my physician greeted us with a smile from ear to ear. I will never know where his boisterous enthusiasm comes from at 6:30 in the morning. However, his energy, excitement, and confidence made us that much more eager to see little Hunter's face for the first time.

To say my first birthing experience didn't happen as I hoped would be an understatement. I wanted to birth Noah without the use of pain medication. However, that little stinker decided to lodge both his head and his ankles under my right rib cage for the last three months of my pregnancy. This bought me a sterile, draped abdominal surgery to get him out. I would be lying if I didn't say I was disappointed that I didn't experience full labor. I felt like I had missed my "rite of passage" as a mother. But, at the end of the day, I was just so incredibly thankful to have safely delivered a healthy baby boy. I love how, even in the growing of Noah, the Creator of life knew best to arrange Noah's tiny body in a breech position. Even then the Lord knew what would be in store during Hunter's birth. On this early morning in July, He knew it would be best if I was surrounded by an anesthesiologist and hooked up to a cardiac monitor. His Sovereignty, His limitless power to do what He decides to do,[1] over Noah's birth was not mutually exclusive from Hunter's birth. God's sovereignty flows and encompasses all.

It was time. . . .

One of the operating room nurses came to lead me back into the operating room. She would prep me for the surgery and hold me steady as the long and not-so-skinny needle was inserted into my back to deliver the spinal block, numbing the entire lower part of my body. Although my heart was beating fast and hard, I felt confident in my physician's ability in performing cesarean sections. After all, I had "been there . . . done that." I knew what to expect. I prayed a little prayer on my walk into the OR, simply saying, "Lord, thank You. Thank You for my boys. Thank You for life. I don't deserve this." I was overcome with gratefulness for the blessings of my marriage and our growing family.

Once all of the drapes were hung and my belly had been scrubbed sterile, John was escorted into the operating room to stand by my side. He held onto my left hand with such warmth. He made me feel secure and safe. My body was cold, and I could not keep both of my arms from shaking what felt like violently. The anesthesiologist placed a nicely warmed blanket on my chest. As the procedure began, I increasingly experienced a feeling of light-headedness. Everything around me turned from such clarity in all of my five senses to one big fuzzy mess. I heard surrounding voices speaking to one another and even to me, but all the words were undistinguishable. It was as if everyone's voice was in the far distant background. Clearly something was not right.

I remember shifting my head to the right to glance at the cardiac monitor because, after all, when you are a nurse, checking the monitor is second nature. Yes, you heard that correctly. A nurse. An ICU nurse. That initial glance turned into a stare. I had just earned my master's degree in nursing, and I had worked in pediatric cardiology in the intensive care unit for the preceding six years. So, when I observed that every other to every third heartbeat was an irregular beat, my fuzzy brain became concerned. At the same time I recall a second anesthesiologist urgently entering the operating room. I then saw my heart rhythm go into ventricular tachycardia. For the nonmedical folks reading this, ventricular tachycardia, or VT, is not a good heart rhythm. If uncorrected by medication or electrical shock, it will lead to death. As my eyes rolled to the back of my head and my eyelids slowly shut, I thought, *They might just have to start CPR on me.*

And . . . time . . . stood . . . still.

In that moment, I experienced something that would take me many months to even speak of aloud. The sounds of the operating room dimmed in my ears to almost a silence, and somehow, all I knew was brightness—complete, surrounding, and all-encompassing brightness. All I knew was a surreal, overpowering peace. All I knew was that I could feel the blood vessels dilate in my body all the way down to my toes. Warmth overcame my entire chilled body. Why was this strange? Because I was medically paralyzed and numb from the waist down for the surgery. I should not have been able to sense anything in my lower body. But I could almost move my toes. The calming peace I experienced cannot be described with words. Truly, there is no way for me to articulate any of this awe-filled, all-consuming peace. In my heart, I believe the Lord covered me with His presence in that very moment. And His presence alone was better than anything this world has to offer. Including my beloved husband. Including my precious little Hunter I had yet to even lay eyes on. Including the precious twenty-month-old who had won my heart and was presently sleeping peacefully miles away in his crib at home.

I do not know how much time passed before I heard the cries of my son, Hunter. I have no memory of my doctor lifting Hunter's freshly born body up in the air for me to see over the drapes that were hung near my chest. I have no idea how long the anesthesiologist tugged on my shoulder to get me to open my eyes. What I do know is that I did not want my eyes to open. I did not want to leave this peace. I did not want to leave the brightness.

The medical team did not need to resuscitate me or perform CPR on me the morning of Hunter's birth. On this particular morning my heart spontaneously reset itself; however, I no doubt created more-than-a-little scare for my ob-gyn. Throughout both of my pregnancies, he teased me that if something was going to go wrong, it seemed that those incidents happened most frequently with other medical professionals. Well, Doc, you were right about that one! But in reality this was the beginning of God's intense pursuit of my soul. None of the events from that July 14, 2009, morning or the many other events over the next few years were one bit outside the Lord's hands or His control.

I often wonder about what happened during that time of complete brightness. Many ask, "Did you experience heaven?" The answer is no. I did not see Jesus face-to-face. I did not see angels. However, I do believe that just because

I did not see our God face-to-face does not mean I did not experience Him. I experienced a peace that was more important to me than saying good-bye to my husband, who happens to be the love of my life and my best friend. I experienced a peace that was more desirable than laying eyes on the precious little boy that was just brought into the world or going home to my sweet Noah. So, although I did not experience heaven, I did experience the One who dwells in heaven. The presence and peace of Jesus were better than my greatest joys on this earth. This feeling was enough; in fact, it was more than enough! His presence birthed an unquenchable longing within the core of my being for my eternal home!

So it may not surprise you that when people ask me to pray over them, I am quick to ask for the Lord's nearness and the Lord's presence. We do not need to die in order to experience Jesus; we just need to stop, pause, and cease striving long enough to need Him, love Him, and rest in Him. God's Word states in Psalm 145:18, "The LORD is near to all who call upon Him, to all who call upon Him in truth" (NASB). His nearness and His presence can truly bring an incomprehensible

> *His presence birthed an unquenchable longing within the core of my being for my eternal home!*

and unexplainable peace in the moments of our greatest sufferings, as well as in the mundane tasks of our waking hours. I simply desire for others to experience Jesus as I did on July 14, 2009, and like I continue to experience Him even in the commonplace, unexciting tasks from day to day, and from hour to hour.

My precious boys,

You are so young and full of energy and life as I write this to you. If the Lord wills, you will have many decades of life to live in front of you. I want you to know that although you may believe that you are self-sufficient, I pray your hearts, minds, and souls will see your need for complete dependence on Jesus. Sometimes the Lord uses the hard things of life to reveal to us our need for Jesus. And this is a blessing . . . that we will be aware of our true need for the Lord. My prayer is that the Lord will birth in you a zealous desire for His Word. I pray that reading through the Bible will remind you of God's promises and remind you of His nearness over your life. Each one of you will come face-to-face with hard and, dare I even say, devastating circumstances throughout your life. I pray that in those moments you will ask . . . no . . . that you will BEG Jesus to be near so that you can sense His presence with you.

When your mind and heart and thoughts and soul are consumed with the Truth of Scripture, Jesus truly pours out over us what is written in Philippians 4:7, "The peace of God, which transcends all understanding, will guard your hearts and minds in Christ Jesus" (NIV). His consuming peace and presence allow us to authentically say to whatever circumstance we face, "It is well with my soul." We can say, "It is well with my soul," not because we agree with the circumstance, not because we believe the suffering is fair and just (for more times than not, we will think the complete opposite). But our soul, our mind, and our heart can experience and embrace His peace because Jesus is the Rock upon which we stand . . . or fall upon, or barely hang onto. Jesus is enough. Shouting His name to the heavens when all is wrong and broken will reveal one's authentic surrender to Him. And, in our surrender to Jesus, He will respond with the grace of His presence and peace. Scripture states in 2 Thessalonians 3:16, "Now may the Lord of peace Himself continually grant you peace in every circumstance" (NASB).

So in this moment I am praying for Jesus to remind you that He loves you and desires for you to call out His name, the name above all names, when you are hurting. Yet not just in your hurting but also in seasons of joy and abundance; for all blessings flow from above, the Giver of life. Boys, may you persevere through this life with not just an occasional need for Jesus but a daily desperation for Jesus.

I love you . . . my heart, mommy

Chapter 2

Not What I Would Have Planned

*"Do not fear, for I am with you;
do not be afraid, for I am your God.
I will strengthen you; I will help you; I will hold
on to you with My righteous right hand."*
ISAIAH 41:10

When Hunter was six weeks of age, John and I went to my first cardiology appointment following the events that occurred at the time of Hunter's birth. This was supposed to be a "normal, routine appointment" where I would hopefully be told that my heart was healthy. The nervous tension grew as I watched the second hand slowly circulate the clock hanging on the wall of the waiting room. I was so nervous that I kept asking John awkward conversation starter questions just to get him to talk, as if listening to his voice would make the wait any less nerve-racking.

John graciously entertained my questions, which if you know my husband, is not surprising. He even responded to the questions for which he knew I already knew the answers. What's funny is that even as John was talking, I wasn't really listening. (Shh! Don't tell him!) Instead, I was having my own inner dialogue. I knew I was having symptoms: shortness of breath walking up a flight of stairs, light-headedness while taking a warm shower, and fatigue when pushing the stroller down the street. However, within the ongoing debate in my mind, I had explained away each one of those symptoms to being an exhausted mother of a newborn, being out of shape from the pregnancy, and likely dehydrated from breast-feeding. Plus, I was now pushing a double stroller that housed nearly fifty pounds of children and their gear. That in itself would make anyone short of breath, right?! I kept telling myself that whatever had happened on that early morning in July was an isolated event. Surely it wasn't anything other than a crazy, one-time set of circumstances.

Then suddenly, mid-conversation, a woman dressed in maroon scrubs appeared from the doorway in the corner of the room saying, "Manning. Manning." Oh, okay, I guess it was my turn. The nervous tingling in my belly intensified. My palms became slightly sweatier. And my heart might as well have been a gymnast by the amount of flip-flopping it was doing inside my chest.

Once escorted back to the exam room, we were greeted by my cardiologist, who offered big smiles and congratulatory hugs to both John and me. She made such sweet compliments regarding tiny Hunter, who was cozily nestled in his car seat. As the conversation shifted from pleasantries to the clinical, she asked how I had been feeling physically, and believe it or not, I shared openly all of my symptoms. I even confessed how I attempted to convince my brain that everything was A-okay. And, honestly, our visit was really not too concerning. The cardiologist suggested that I have one more test performed on my heart, an echocardiogram or sonogram of the heart muscle, "just to make sure everything was okay." The sonographer came to get me from the exam room almost immediately, for which I was thankful. Hunter would need to be fed shortly, and he would be certain to voice his cries for Mommy's milk.

The lights were dimmed in the room where I changed into a hospital gown. In fact, the only real source of light in the room was originating from the echocardiogram machine. As I gently lowered myself down on the bed, slightly rotating onto my left side, the sonographer asked me why I was seeing the cardiologist. I broadly shared the details from Hunter's birth as John interjected other details I had forgotten. Truth be told, John has and always will be the better storyteller between the two of us. Our conversation with the sonographer was truly a welcome source of distraction for me, as I really did not want to look at the images of my heart for fear my eyes just might see something wrong. I desired the expertise of my cardiologist to make conclusions about how my heart muscle was functioning and not my own novice eyes. Before we knew it, the test was completed, and I was redressing just in time for Hunter to make known that his belly was indeed empty.

In the medical world we like to say, "No news is good news." Test results are typically communicated once several days have passed and the nurse in the office has had a chance to return all of the emergent phone calls that filter through to her. My expectations were that John and I could leave the cardiology office and exhale, knowing that we would learn the findings within the next few days. All we could do was wait.

Isn't it ironic how we often go through each day of our lives relying on our own knowledge, our own strength, and our own power? Most of us believe we could control the details of our own life, our spouse's life, and the lives of our children. Up to this point in my career, I had spent the last six years working as a nurse taking care of children born with heart defects. I would care for them in the pediatric intensive care unit as they recovered from open-heart surgery. I had just enough medical knowledge of what went on the day Hunter was born to create a false sense of security in knowing that I did not hold the typical risk factors for having heart disease. "I am going to be fine," I told myself. "I exercise, eat healthy, and know how to pay attention to my body's symptoms. I have run long distances and gained a healthy amount of weight during the pregnancy. I am going to be fine."

I had only been home for about half an hour—just long enough to say good-bye to our babysitter and get both boys settled into place—when I heard our home phone ringing. The caller ID read: "ADC Clinic." I caught myself holding my breath, and as I cautiously answered the phone, my heart began to pound violently within my chest.

"Hello?" I answered meekly.

"Yes, is this Julie?" the woman replied.

"Yes, this is she."

"Hi, Julie. This is Dr. Anderson."

My heart sank deep into my chest. I had worked in the medical field long enough to know the news I was about to receive was not going to be good. No, the news was *not* going to be reassuring. How did I know this? Well, not only was I receiving the result of my echocardiogram within a mere hour of the test's performance, but also my physician (not her nurse or her medical assistant or the receptionist) had dialed my phone number to deliver the news *herself*.

She warmly and compassionately said, "Julie, you may want to sit down for this conversation."

The pause on the other end of the phone felt as if it lasted an eternity. What words would follow?

"Julie, I reviewed your echocardiogram with several of my colleagues in order to confirm what I was seeing. We all agree that your heart is not functioning well. I am sorry to say, you are in heart failure."

Heart. Failure?

The words echoed in my mind as I sank deeper into the chair. Heart failure? Really?! Dr. Anderson continued to share more detailed findings of the test as I found my eyes scanning the room to find Hunter peacefully asleep in the bouncy chair and Noah intently working on putting together floor puzzles next to the sofa. I probably should have been writing down every syllable of every word she was sharing, but all I could do was stare at my two baby boys, unable to move my focus from their precious little bodies to the pencil and pad of paper that were shaking in my hands.

I hung up the phone and just sat there motionless. As my mind and my emotions were battling to make sense of it all, I found myself paralyzed by the news. After a few moments I knew I needed to call John. With tears welling up in my eyes, I phoned him at work and recounted as much of the conversation as I could remember.

August 26, 2009

Lord, you are humbling me. My weaknesses are showing, and I am learning I am indeed not Superwoman. I cannot go through this life without You and the help of others. I received a phone call yesterday afternoon that my heart is failing. What???!!! I am really in complete shock, and I feel like I am talking about someone else. Not me. Not me—not the girl who takes care of herself. Not the athlete. Not the one who cares for others on the brink of death in the hospital. I'm supposed to be the one caring for others, not be the one being cared for.

Lord, I am scared. Really scared.

Yet somehow, almost ironically, I remain hopeful. This hope must be coming from You because I cannot muster up hope of my own right now.

I want to see my boys grow up. I do not want to leave them! I am their mommy. I want to be here for them. I want to teach them how to tie shoes and ride bicycles without training wheels, to nervously watch them drive a car at sixteen, and to hold their babies one day. Lord, Noah isn't even two years old yet! Hunter is only six weeks old. I want to spend as much time as possible with them and my John.

The Bible shares many stories about the miraculous healing that occurred through the hands of Jesus and His disciples by faith. Will You give me the faith to believe that You are my healer—both this side of heaven and IN heaven. I do believe You care about my life and about my boys' lives. I know You are a God of compassion and understanding. I believe You created me, and You are not surprised one bit by these circumstances. I lean into that right now.

Jesus, forgive me for not seeking You as I should. Forgive me of my pride that I think I can go through this life without really and truly relying on my Savior. I need you. I need my Savior, Redeemer, Healer. Be my Rock. Be my Strength. Be my everything!

I ask that You heal my heart and that You get ALL the glory from it. I ask that You use the medicine I just started taking to help strengthen my myocardial fibers to contract effectively and efficiently. I ask that during this time YOU will be my story . . . that the focus of all conversations will be of and about You. I need Your grace and mercy. Strengthen John. Make him steadfast. Amen.

You are a God of compassion and understanding.

God answered my prayer for John long before I even prayed asking Jesus to make him steadfast. See, John is indeed steadfast. He has been steadfast since the beginning of our marriage. He remained faithful and steady through our miscarriage and times of financial uncertainties. And this time John stood unshaken as I withdrew daily, well almost daily, to take a shower. The shower transformed into my hiding place, where I felt safe to fall on my face and have a good ole ugly cry. It would not be fair of me to solely place blame on my postpartum hormones for these episodes of uncontrollable crying. Although I am sure they added to my emotional swings. But with all honesty I was flat-out scared my life would end up being much shorter than I had planned. Key words: "I had planned." Frankly, I felt out of control. Completely out of control! In an effort to control at least something, I began searching for anything I could control. Let's just say, it was a failed attempt.

After a few days had passed, John and I decided to seek a second opinion. In hindsight, I feel pretty naïve and ridiculously illogical as I truly hoped for better news as we entered the office of Dr. Ferguson. I was REALLY hoping the first cardiologist was flat-out wrong. However, not only did Dr. Ferguson agree with the diagnosis, but she also matter-of-factly shared that only time would tell how my heart would respond to medication. My heart function could stay the same (may I remind you they had labeled my heart function with the term "failing"), my heart muscle might begin to repair itself with the aid of medication (Yes, Lord, I would love this option!), or it might progressively worsen over time. Of those three options the third scenario led us into an intense discussion of the logistics of being placed on the heart-transplant waiting list. Yet, "only time would tell." Only Jesus would know my outcome.

In time we would know the plan Jesus would have for my physical heart, for my life, and for the sanctification of my soul. Ultimately, He would use this sudden suffering in my life to prune the pride, the control, and the comfort from my life and replace it with increasing faith in Him, His Word, His promises, and His unchanging, unwavering character.

So, what did the doctors know with certainty? At that moment in time, my heart had been damaged, and scar tissue was developing. Scar tissue can disrupt the electrical conduction of a heart's rhythmic beating just like roadblocks lead to detours; however, my scar tissue— my detours—not only cause rerouted traffic patterns but also sometimes act like traffic circles where you are trapped on the inside lane and unable to exit. Thus, you find yourself going 'round and 'round and 'round again. Sort of like the well-known movie quote from *European Vacation*, starring Chevy Chase, "Look kids! Big Ben. Parliament!" Dr. Ferguson could not say with certainty if I would or would not experience a potentially dangerous heart rhythm. I had to wait until an electrophysiologist, a specialized cardiologist that focuses solely on the electrical activities of the heart, could evaluate me. Thankfully, an electrophysiologist could see me the next day.

If that was not enough information for my brain to try to digest, our discussion turned to a more sensitive topic. Without missing a beat or changing the inflection in her voice, Dr. Ferguson rather firmly stated, "Julie, describe your plans for birth control because you will *not* have future pregnancies." Wow! Okay. Can we all agree that this was a lot. I just learned that we cannot predict whether my heart function will improve or if I will eventually need a heart transplant. I also learned my heart rhythm has the potential to go into a dangerous, life-threatening heart rhythm due to scar tissue. To top it all off, I am told my body cannot bear any more children due to the likelihood I would not survive the pregnancy, let alone the immediate postpartum season. If I were in a boxing ring, I am pretty sure this would have been the final punch causing a knockout. Ding! White flag is raised.

Now in all reality we had our tiny, healthy baby Hunter at home, attempting miserably to sleep a consistent four- to five-hour stretch during the night. With this precious six-week-old at home, family planning was not really at the forefront of my mind; survival was. I knew I might want more children eventually, but this was not a priority for me in the present season. My spirit was overwhelmingly thankful for the two precious boys the Lord allowed my body to birth. I would eventually grieve this piece of fertility news but not on this particular afternoon. Rather, on this day, I just wanted to remain off the heart-transplant waiting list. I just wanted to stay alive through the night, into the next day, and hopefully—yes, hopefully—long enough to see my youngest turn one year of age.

I am overwhelmingly thankful for Dr. Ferguson. The Lord brought her into our lives, and I could not imagine walking through this journey without her medical wisdom and true passion for her patients. I have not once walked into her office and not felt her fighting on my behalf. Yes, she has always spoken directly and not beaten around the bush, and for this I am grateful. John describes himself as the eternal optimist. It is true. He really is. Yet I am a realist, and I wanted to know the fight I was facing. She clearly let me know that I was the underdog. It was okay. I have a heart for the underdog.

Boys,

Simply put, God is who He says He is. Our sufferings do not produce belief or unbelief of the Lord in our lives; rather our sufferings will reveal our belief or unbelief in Jesus. Noah and Hunter, you both were so tiny when Mommy and Daddy faced all of this news. I am so thankful you were protected from seeing the chaos that was consuming my mind and my heart during these initial weeks. I shed more tears those first few weeks than I had over decades. However, I want all of you to know how real the shock and chaos was. I want you to know that I struggled with a consuming fear of leaving this earth before you really knew me as Mommy. I also want you to know that Jesus, in His faithfulness, calmed my fears and multiplied my trust in Him that He never leaves or abandons those who believe in Him.

I want you to know that you, too, will likely experience sudden, life-changing news one day. There will likely be a day when you feel you have been thrown into the ocean and you are unable to see the shore. I pray your hearts and minds know that there is One constant . . . One who is ever present . . . One who knows the smallest of details in your life . . . One that foreknew the chaos for which your life would be exposed. You are never alone, though you might try to convince yourself otherwise. I pray you will be steadfast like your Daddy. I pray you will lean on the Truth of God's Word when these times come. I pray that you will be able to hold your wife in your arms and remind her that Jesus is with you and that His nearness is for our good. Yes, your Mommy was scared, and sometimes that fear creeps back into my thoughts. In fact, Hunter, when you ask Mommy why she gets tears in her eyes while watching you build Legos or play soccer or color me a picture, it is because I am trying to soak up every second I have with you. However, I am daily choosing to trust the Word of God over my fears and uncertainties. In this I find freedom and peace to live for today and not worry about what tomorrow holds. I pray this over your lives, that the Lord will give you increasingly more faith day by day, trial by trial, season by season.

May you remember what is written in Isaiah 55:8–9: "'For My thoughts are not your thoughts, and your ways are not My ways.' This is the LORD's declaration. 'For as heaven is higher than earth, so *My ways are higher than your ways, and My thoughts than your thoughts.'*"

Trust in our unchanging God . . . *whose ways are higher . . . whose ways have eternal purposes . . . whose ways are always trustworthy.*

my heart, mommy

Chapter 3

The Valley

Even when I go through the darkest valley,
I fear no danger, for You are with me;
Your rod and Your staff—they comfort me."
PSALM 23:4

Two weeks after we discovered that my heart was failing, I found myself in the hospital once again. Dr. Mills, my electrophysiologist, believed I was an excellent candidate for a procedure called an ablation. A cardiac ablation establishes appropriately and strategically placed roadblocks to stop the abnormal electrical signals from traveling through the heart muscle. This otherwise routine procedure, as some would call it, would hopefully put a stop to my irregular heart rhythms and make it safer for me to walk around in the outside world away from the four walls of a hospital where medications and defibrillators are within an arm's reach. Dr. Mills then referred us to the physician in his group that specialized in ablating ventricular arrhythmias, or irregular rhythms originating from the bottom two chambers of the heart.

Once again, John and I had an early morning wake-up call for a drive to the hospital. Except this time we were both already up and moving because little Hunter wanted to eat around 4:00 a.m. His sweet cries and pleas to stay awake and party rather than fall back asleep aroused John from his slumber.

John and I strolled into the rather small hospital waiting room at 5:57 a.m. The room was already crowded. Yet so quiet you could hear a pin drop. We whispered, "Good morning," to the receptionist and signed in. We found the only two remaining unoccupied seats and plopped down. I placed my head on his right shoulder and happily rested my eyes. After a few moments passed and a few short glances around the room, John and I turned to look at each other and smiled with our eyes. We both noticed it at the same time. Every other person sitting in the waiting room was at least four decades ahead of us in life. We were surrounded by a group of people who had lived a lot of life. One sweet little lady in particular struck up a conversation with John while I was called back up to the receptionist's desk. This barely five-foot-tall woman leaned over the arm of her chair and began to compliment John, saying how lovely it was that we would awaken before dawn to come be with our family members during the heart procedure. I do not blame her one bit for jumping to that conclusion. We could have passed for the grandchildren of every last person in the room. Sweet John offered a gentle smile and graciously told her that it was actually his wife that was having an ablation and not his grandfather. Oh, that sweet woman! Here she was accompanying her husband of four decades, and John and I were still in our "honeymoon years."

On that day I would stand out to Dr. Hanks for multiple reasons. The first one obviously being demographic. I was only thirty-two years old, not seventy-two. Second, I asked to meet him face-to-face in the preoperative area before going under anesthesia. The expeditious time frame of scheduling my procedure did not afford me the opportunity of meeting with Dr. Hanks in his outpatient office prior to that morning. So I became *the* high-maintenance patient who might just have caused a delay in his schedule due to my request. Please accept my sincere apologies, Dr. Hanks. Third, and most comically (in my opinion), my standing out had everything to do with the fact that his first impression of me happened to include his entering my preoperative room to a full frontal view of yours truly attached to the breast pump. Since I was still able to breast-feed Hunter on my heart-failure medications, I figured I might as well provide Hunter with another bottle or two of milk rather than leak (I mean shoot) breast milk all over the operating table. Yes, please chuckle. I do, just thinking about it. And, come on, you mommas reading this know what I mean! However, while I believe I made the most memorable first impression, I guarantee Dr. Hanks will knock before entering a lactating mother's room next time.

The Lord was so sweet to us by providing moments of joy and laughter on this early morning. From the waiting room to the initial introduction of the physician, John and I found joy in a day where the outcome would be significantly different from our expectations. Isn't that just like God? If we just surrender to Him and begin to observe this world with an eternal perspective, a Jesus perspective, then our hearts might find joy despite the crazy circumstances in which we find ourselves living.

Shortly after our brief and extremely awkward hellos, I was wheeled down the fluorescent-lit hallway to the electrophysiology (EP) lab where Dr. Hanks planned to perform the EP study and ablation. Entering the EP lab felt like going into a spaceship from a science-fiction movie. The lights were dimmed to the lowest setting. At least five or six huge computer monitor screens to my left would display data and electrical-

> *If we just surrender to Him and begin to observe this world with an eternal perspective, then our hearts might find joy despite our current life circumstances.*

mapping information in a rainbow of colors. The nurse sensed that I was becoming increasingly nervous. I am not sure if it was my poor attempt of creating laughter in the room or the jitterness of my hands that was the dead giveaway. Have I mentioned that I am NOT the comedian of the family?! She then began asking me questions about my family. As I shared about Noah, Hunter, and John, my heart rate began to slow. The anesthesiologist for the procedure then entered the room and introduced himself. He got to work quickly, and somewhere along the way, I "fell asleep" midsentence while asking the nurse about her own family.

It is always a strange feeling to "fall asleep" under anesthesia. You go from being anxious about the procedure to feeling extremely relaxed, without a care in the world about what is about to happen. Not only that, but you do not remember anything that happened as your heavy eyelids peel open to find yourself in a completely different location from your last memory. On that day, as my fractionally opened eyes received glimpses of sunlight from the window in the corner of the room, I knew I had made it through the procedure. As foggy as my brain was in that moment, I somehow noticed John was sitting to my right with his two hands clasped, supporting his bowed head. The room was eerily silent and extremely bright from the midday sun. As I moved my gaze to look at him, he slowly lifted his head. I could feel the strength of his two hands as he moved to gently embrace my right hand. He softly spoke, "I love you. Dr. Hanks said he would be in to speak with us once you were awake."

And that he did—not more than fifteen minutes later. The stoic, self-confident, and almost robotic man I had met just hours before entered the room with a much more compassionate demeanor. He pulled up a chair and sat at the foot of the bed, crossing his legs at his ankles. As he made eye contact, he let out an audible exhale. Dr. Hanks shared that when he was mapping out the electric pathways within my heart, he found more than ten locations where premature, or early, ventricular beats were originating. He was hoping to only find one. He went on to explain that because of this it was not feasible for him to ablate all of the locations, for this would have created too many areas of additional scarring to the muscle tissue, and I had already developed areas of scarring due to my heart failure. Simply put, the more scar tissue within the heart, the more likely a lethal or deadly arrhythmia could happen. Dr. Hanks continued to elucidate that with the combination of my poorly squeezing heart muscle and the presence of nearly a dozen origination spots for a ventricular arrhythmia, I was at an increased risk for a sudden cardiac death. He then highly encouraged me to have an implantable cardiac defibrillator (ICD) placed into my chest immediately—as in the very next morning.

An ICD is a medical device with the capability to monitor every single heartbeat a heart generates. The ICD is programmed to recognize when a lethal heart rhythm exists. If and when this occurs, the ICD will then administer an electrical shock to the heart with the hopes that the heart rhythm will reset itself back to normal. If you grew up watching the television show *ER* or even *Grey's Anatomy*, just think of the scenes when two big paddles were placed on patients' chests and everyone shouted, "CLEAR!" However, the "paddles" of the ICD are actually screwed (yes, screwed) into the heart muscle wall. The device (for which these internal paddles are connected) that monitors and houses the battery power to deliver an intense shock is half the size of an iPhone and is implanted under the left chest wall.

Having worked in the area of cardiology and been the bedside nurse for hundreds of pediatric patients postoperatively from heart surgeries and ICD and pacemaker placements, I understood what Dr. Hanks inferred as he calmly and even sympathetically shared his recommendations. Our discussion lasted nearly forty-five minutes, and Dr. Hanks patiently answered all of our questions and listened to our concerns as we attempted to wrap our minds around the urgency and gravity of the situation. We asked if we could have some time to talk, and he graciously obliged. However, Dr. Hanks urged us not to take too much time in making the decision.

One of my colleagues from graduate school had already begun working for one of the pediatric electrophysiologists in town. When I texted her the outcome of the morning's procedure, she mentioned that Dr. Marshall would be happy to spend time speaking with us to answer any questions that remained. We did not for one second hesitate on that offer. Within several minutes of Dr. Hanks exiting my hospital room, I was on the phone with Dr. Marshall. I shared with him what we had been told regarding the outcome of the electrophysiology study. Dr. Marshall matter-of-factly shared that, if I were his patient, he would not delay in implanting an ICD. With this input John and I gained confidence in the decision we knew we needed to make. We informed my bedside nurse that afternoon of our decision to have the ICD placed the next morning.

At the time everything seemed so technical, and the decisions being made were decided merely with the intellectual facets of our brain. In those hours I felt extremely disconnected emotionally. I am good at putting on my "medical hat," walling off my emotions, and making crucial decisions in emergency situations. I truly credit my nursing experience and mentors in the pediatric intensive care unit (PICU) for this skill set. For when a child's health began to deteriorate rapidly, I knew my role and stepped up to perform tasks needed to help save a life. The only difference? This time I was the patient. And I really did not know how to reconcile the medical with the emotional. I did not know how I was supposed to react as the patient and not the medical provider. The only thing I knew for certain was that I had a desperate desire to hold my baby boys.

Several hours passed, and John and I were able to place a few phone calls to spread the word asking for prayer. Friends began texting us Scriptures pointing us to the Truth of God's Word and His goodness. Slowly the hospital room transitioned from being a cold, unadorned room with four bare walls, IV poles, and cardiac monitors, to a noticeable place of warmth and feeling as if we were not alone. And the truth is that we are never alone. Psalm 23:4 states, "Even when I go through the darkest valley, I fear no danger, for You are with me; Your rod and Your staff—they comfort me." This was my valley, and I was not alone.

One of the kind nurses who prepped me for the procedure in the EP lab earlier that morning stopped by my room to check on me at the end of her shift. She took a seat on the bed near my feet as we visited. Her genuine kindness, compassion, and concern facilitated an easy but vulnerable conversation. She asked how our conversation went with Dr. Hanks. I was confident she knew of the impending ICD placement. How could she not after being present for the entire EP study? Regardless, I shared with her that we had decided to have the ICD placed the following morning. Her body language conveyed her support of our decision. I also asked her about the large, rectangular red marks I noticed on my chest. I thought my skin was sensitive to the sticker pads she had placed on me just hours earlier prior to the procedure. This sweet woman's eyes began to glisten as she slowly shook her head no. Her hand gently reached out to touch my ankle, which was tucked underneath the covers. Her eyes alone led me to believe that she did not want to be the one sharing the details of what had happened. I believe she had hoped Dr. Hanks might have told us, but alas, it was her voice that would echo in my mind for years.

"No, Sweetie, those are not from the stickers. Those red marks are burns. We had to shock you." She repeated herself, "We had to shock you twice."

I had to be shocked?! Twice?!

My heart sank into my stomach. Silence overtook the conversation. I didn't know how or even if I was to respond. What other surprises would today hold? I just sat there with such a vivid image in my mind of what had occurred in the EP lab. I had anticipated I would come through this routine procedure unscathed. I mean, the only thing different I could have anticipated for the OR staff was leaking breast milk all over the operating room table.

While working as a nurse in the PICU, I participated in resuscitations of children. I, too many times, have witnessed tiny children's bodies being lifted off the hospital bed due to the intensity of the shock administered to their chests. I have stood over their bodies delivering chest compressions wondering if their little hearts would begin to beat on their own again. Yet this time the image was not of a child. This time I visualized my own body being lifted off the table. Not just once—but twice.

Twice means the first shock did not work. Twice means my heart was not pumping blood and thus oxygen to the rest of my body. Twice means all the members of the medical team in the room held their breath hoping the second shock delivered would actually stimulate my heart to spontaneously beat in an organized manner. Twice means the anesthesiologist was preparing medications to administer in a "code." Twice means without intervention I was headed to meet my Maker.

Suddenly my emotions were engaged. Suddenly I began to realize that we really were not just talking about another patient or medical scenario . . . but my own heart . . . my own life . . . my own breath.

_____
This life is truly just a breath.
_____

And this life is truly just that . . . a breath.

Boys,

All that flows out of my heart right now is "I love you." I want to say it to you a million times over again. And I so desperately want you to know that Jesus loves you even more. He loves you all the way to the cross. He is always with you. He is always near. He will hear every cry, every whisper, and every word you say to Him. You do not travel through this life alone . . . not on the mountainous climbs, the steady walks, or the deepest of valleys traversed. He is always with you and, thus, you should have nothing to fear. This life will be hard, but God promises in Psalm 23:4 to be with you, with us, as we walk through the valley of the shadow of death. Because God is who He says He is. . . . Because God is unchanging, you can find peace and hope for the eternal, in both the good and the hard of this life. I pray for God's nearness over your lives. May you always beg God for His nearness to be known over your hearts and minds. . . . In every situation, every circumstance, every breath.

I love you . . . to heaven and back.

my heart, mommy

Chapter 4

Life Is a Breath

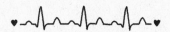

"LORD, reveal to me the end of my life and the number of my days. Let me know how short-lived I am. You, indeed, have made my days short in length, and my life span as nothing in Your sight. Yes, every mortal man is only a vapor. Selah."

PSALM 39:4–5

Every man at his best is a mere breath. On September 30 and again on October 1, 2009, my heart stopped. Each day a shock would be delivered that would not revive me. However, the Lord would graciously use the second shocks to breathe life back into my body, causing my heart to beat in a normal rhythm. On both of those particular days, God was not ready for me to enter heaven. But one day this is certain, He WILL bring me home.

October 7, 2009

Lord, you are showing me more than I ever thought I could learn, in a baptism-by-fire kind of way. Just eight days ago I faced death on the table. Then my body became momentarily lifeless again the following day. Why did you choose to breathe life into me again and again? You could have easily snatched me up into heaven, but You did not.

I have moments during the day when I truly feel covered in peace. I think (in those moments) I feel a little crazy that I have peace. The world tells me I should be scared of death and that I should be falling into self-pity and depression. Do not be fooled, I have many hours of that, too. But in this moment I have peace, probably because I am currently spending time with You. And this peace I have is not something I have self-generated. It is a peace that comes from knowing there is more to this life than what the world chooses to see.

I am so thankful for every moment of every day. Every smile on Noah and Hunter's faces, every touch of their little but growing hands, give me such joy. Every conversation and moment I have with John is an added blessing. I truly love these three boys so much. I cannot imagine life without them, and I also cannot imagine leaving them behind. Yet, Lord, help me to trust that You will give John the strength, that You will give John the daily grace and mercy, that You will give John the support through friends and family to not only make it, but experience Your joy when I am gone from this earth and my side of our bed is empty. Help me to trust that You alone will be John's everything.

Cause my hope to be found in You alone. I desperately pray for Noah and Hunter that they will grow up to be men of integrity, men that seek to live for Your kingdom, and men that cling to the Scriptures. Jeremiah 29:13 states, "You will seek Me and find Me when you search for Me with all your heart." And in Psalm 27:8–9, David, a man after Your own heart, beautifully depicts the ongoing dialogue between the mind and the heart, "My heart says this about You, 'You are to seek My face.' Lord, I will seek Your face. Do not hide Your face from me; do not turn Your servant away in anger. You have been my helper; do not leave me or abandon me, God of my salvation." I cling to these words right now. Too often I will independently process Your Word by either using intellect or by using my emotive heart, but not both at the same time. In this moment I am witnessing the beauty of using both intellect and heart simultaneously. Yes, Lord, I will. I am seeking Your face, Your nearness, Your presence.

These circumstances are weighty, Lord. My days are numbered. I no longer merely understand this in theory, but I am living this out in reality. Life is too brief. Your Word says life is a vapor. And, for the remainder of my days here on earth, I will seek Your face, Your name, and Your glory. You are my Creator, the Creator of all things, and You are my Savior. You died on the cross for my sin, and yet You even conquered death. Death did not hold you down. When You rose from the grave, You revealed Yourself to many as You spent forty days walking around on the earth ministering to Your disciples before ascending back into heaven, Your dwelling place and Your home. In a way I feel like You have given me a little added bonus time here on the earth, whether it be forty days or forty years, to finish up the work You desire for me to complete. So, Lord, show me what You desire for and from my life while I am still here on Earth. Show me how I can impact my family and my community while You still give me breath. I believe You have a purpose for me; otherwise You would have brought me home. I do not want to waste a single breath, and I do not want my life to be in vain. Use me for some sort of eternal significance, Lord, because I kind of want to be back in the bright light of Your presence. I just want to be home.

I dare to say that our lives are more fragile than each of us probably realizes or truthfully admits. If we are honest with ourselves, we feel confidently secure that when we lay our head on our pillow at night, we will awaken to face another day. We do our best to control the variables in our lives with the hope that we can control our fitness level and health and even avoid obvious risky behaviors. But the truth of the matter is that we are all on borrowed time. If we take time to read the Bible, we are reminded that life this side of heaven is fleeting, even transient. And, if our lives are transient and the things of this world are transient, I sure do want to find something to anchor my soul that does *not* change and is *not* transient. First Peter 1:24–25 points me to the Unchangeable: "For 'all flesh is like grass, and all its glory like the flower of grass. The grass withers, and the flower falls off, but the word of the Lord abides

> *I dare to say that our lives are more fragile than each of us probably realizes or truthfully admits.*

forever.'" The word *abide* used in this verse is the Greek word *meno*, which means "to remain, endure, stand firm, to last."[2] The Word of the Lord, the Bible, remains through all things, endures through all times, stands firm against all circumstances, and will be lasting even until Christ's return for His people.

From the beginning of creation the Lord has numbered my days, and He has numbered your days, your heartbeats, and your breath, too. Each one of us that walks on this earth has been given an appointed time to live and to die. Solomon reminds us in Ecclesiastes 3:1–2, "There is an occasion for everything, and a time for every activity under heaven: a time to give birth and a time to die; a time to plant and a time to uproot." Even though I have been given a diagnosis, my life is no different from yours because the God of creation has designed each one of my breaths just as He has your own. Each of our lives is held in the all-powerful, all-knowing hand of our Creator.

The Word of the Lord, the Bible, remains through all things, endures through all times, stands firm against all circumstances, and will be lasting even until Christ's return for His people.

You may not be constantly reminded of your life's brevity as I am. See, I am reminded hundreds, if not thousands, of times a day when I physically feel my heart flip-flop in my chest, when I become short of breath climbing a flight of stairs, and when I twice daily take the medications to support my heart function. Even with these reminders, I often wonder: *Do I really get it?! Do we really get it?!* What would our lives look like if we really did live with our life's brevity at the forefront of our mind? Would we pursue the temporary, or would we pursue the eternal? I hope my answer is the latter. I have grown to be thankful for the racing heart and skipped heartbeats I feel, for this reminds me that this life is not my own. This life is not about Julie. This life is about living for the One who sacrificed it all on the cross. I owe Him my life, and it is for Him that I desire to live.

My perspective of this life has changed. Friends that knew me before all of this happened would say that I really do live differently. However, this does not mean I am any less prone to reverting back into my old habits or old ways of doing things . . . sinning. I relate to Robert Robinson who penned the words of the well-known hymn "Come Thou Fount of Every Blessing." The hymn was written in 1757. Out of the overflow of Robert's heart, at the young age of twenty-two, came, "Prone to wander Lord I feel it, Prone to leave the God I love. Take my heart Lord, take and seal it. Seal it for Thy courts above." When fear creeps back in my mind or my hands reach out to take hold of control in some area of my life, I am prone to wander. I am prone to wander when I succumb to the tendency of depending on my own self and my own strength and my own abilities, to live out this life apart from the power and promises of God. Yet I am thankful for the Holy Spirit in my life who does not allow me to get that far lost in the forest before my mind and heart are reminded of God's character and His promises that He is faithful to keep— thus, bringing me back to relying on Him for everything.

My diagnosis and my daily symptoms have caused me to be that much more sensitive to living a purposeful and intentional life rather than a life of self-absorption and comparison. When my time does come for me to meet God Almighty, Abba Father, face-to-face, I hope He finds me on the floor reading books to my kids, playing chase in the backyard, or having an authentic and vulnerable conversation with my neighbor. I share this journey, my story with you, with the expectation that Jesus might just use it to impact your life. I earnestly pray for you as your eyes read these words and your heart and mind process what I share. I pray that Jesus will reawaken your soul, giving you the perspective that this place, this earth, is not our forever home. And, because this is not our home, we can face life's circumstances with strength and courage, even grace and joy. Because Jesus is better and because Jesus is enough!

To my sweet boys!

My biggest prayer over your life is that Jesus will awaken you to faith. I pray you will recognize that you need a Savior, and through reading the Scriptures, your mind and heart will agree that Jesus is the true Messiah. The life we are given here on this earth is a vapor. Each day is given to you by the Lord, and it should not be wasted. I pray that you will authentically worship God the Father and Jesus the Son, and I pray the Holy Spirit will fall on you with power. I also pray that the Holy Spirit will help you keep perspective on this life here on the earth. I pray that you will know that this life is not about you, your career advancement, your friends, your athletic pursuits, or even making much of your own name. I pray you will serve others with your life rather than desiring to be served. I pray you will worship the one true God who fulfills rather than the fleeting things of this world that only leave behind a sense of emptiness. I pray that Jesus will persevere you in the faith until the day He brings you home. May your lives be lived with intentionality, purpose, and joy because of Christ. I love you. Boy, do I love you.

my heart, mommy

Chapter 5

Raging War

"My spirit is weak within me; my heart is overcome with dismay. I remember the days of old; I meditate on all You have done; I reflect on the work of Your hands. I spread out my hands to You; I am like parched land before You. Selah."
PSALM 143:4–6

You need to know that I am not Superwoman. I am not some courageous warrior or faith giant. I am not even someone who has "everything together" the vast majority of the time. I am just an ordinary girl who believes she needs a Savior. The Lord allowed these medical circumstances to occur and even allowed me to go through a period of darkness following my diagnosis. I like to call it "wandering in the wilderness with a blindfold covering my eyes and with earplugs in my ears." Because the darkness was in fact quiet, isolating, and lonely.

For you to have a glimpse into the raging war going on inside me, I must share the second half of what was written in my journal on October 7, 2009. I believe it displays the internal wrestling between the soul and the human heart. We all feel the tug-of-war, right? The soul longs to trust Jesus with every fiber of its being, and yet the human heart is fragile and untrusting. My human heart became stuck in a deep, dark pit of fear. The fear and darkness consumed me, sometimes just for a few hours in a given day and other times for multiple days at a time. In my own efforts I attempted to ignore it. I attempted to pretend the darkness did not exist. But it did. And any fight I had within me of my own strength was quickly overtaken by fear and darkness.

> *I attempted to pretend the darkness did not exist. But it did.*

October 7, 2009 (continued)

Jesus, I have to be real; many moments throughout the day scare me. I mean, really scare me. Too often moments exist where fears enter my heart and consume my mind. The times when my heart feels a little crazy—beating funny, palpitating, pockets of air trapped in my chest from my ICD surgery, and feeling the metal underneath my skin. I wonder if and when the ICD will shock me. Will I collapse in front of the kids? Will I be alone? Will I drop to the ground with Noah unable to awaken me? Will it scare the boys? Heck yeah, it would frighten them! Lord, we had to teach Noah to dial 9-1-1. Who teaches their twenty-three-month-old son how to dial 9-1-1?! Forgive me for my unbelief. Forgive me that I do not fully rest in the power of who You say You are. You healed many people as recorded in the Bible. Do I have the faith that You will completely heal my heart? No, honestly, I don't. I want to pray in faith. I want to pray in the name of Jesus that You will restore my heart function. I want to pray You will resolve my cardiomyopathy in a supernatural way. I want to pray and believe that the pathology of my ectopy would disappear. But I am scared to pray with faith because what if you say, "No, that is not My plan for you." What if I pray for healing and You do not show up and heal? I trust that You have the ability to touch my heart and in an instant restore it to a perfect, healthy state. I feel like I have, for some time now, believed that You are ABLE to do this, but I have not been convinced that You WILL. I am scared to start praying that You will heal me because what if you don't?

God, I know You love me. I am your child, and I believe You have a purpose for my life. I believe that my impact here is not complete. You desire to use me, Lord. Make clear the ways You desire to use me, healed or not healed. Help me to trust in Your hand on my life. Forgive me for wanting to control the number of my days. The number of my days rests in Your hands, not mine. And this scares me right now. I feel completely out of control of all areas of my life.

I do love You, Jesus. Help me trust You. Forgive my unbelief. Show me how You desire to be my everything. I need Your peace in the midst of my fears and this darkness. I need You to pull me out of this downward spiral into depression. I need to believe You are true and that Your Word is true.

my heart, julie.

Just days prior to writing these words, I welcomed our friend and pastor, Matt Carter, to our home. He came to visit with us and pray over John and me. As the three of us sat at our kitchen table that cool and overcast morning in October, Matt was kind to share glimpses of what the Lord had shown him through his journey battling appendix cancer several years before. He exhorted me by telling me what a blessing it is to desperately need Jesus for everything and how it was a gift to have everything taken out of my hands of control lest I live my life fully on self-reliance. He sincerely encouraged me to journal, to record every raw emotion and thought down on paper. I remember Matt clearly and authoritatively stating that this season of my life might just be one of the sweetest seasons with the Lord because of how much my eyes saw my absolute, desperate need for Jesus. And, yes, Matt was correct. But I do not want this desperation for Christ to be merely an isolated season that fluctuates with the wind. My hope is that I will continue to feel the weight of complete dependence on Christ as each day of my life stacks on the previous day and weeks turn into months and months turn into years.

I did take Matt's advice. I located a blank journal on the shelf in my closet. I dusted it off and began to write, albeit inconsistently. God spoke His truth through Matt that day. In writing this book, I have once again dusted off the journals I had filled. But this time to reread them. I had not read through them since the days they were written, mostly because I honestly did not want to relive or *refeel* the emotions from that season. My emotions were so incredibly raw. I like to live life looking forward, not looking back at the past. But there has been something beautiful to see in hindsight. Jesus was near to me in the dark season even though at the time I felt so utterly alone.

My journals expressed feelings of loneliness and inadequacy as a mother and wife. I articulated how my thoughts of leaving my sweet

I can now see Jesus' nearness in the midst of such a dark season.

baby boys at an age where they would not remember me caused paralyzing fear.

October 6, 2009

Lord, I am sitting here lost in spiraling thoughts of self-pity. The restrictions placed on me from the surgery do not allow me to pick up Hunter for the next six weeks. I have to have someone place him in my arms to feed him. Someone else has to burp him, change him, bathe him. I am not allowed to lift Noah out of his crib, wrestle with him on the floor to change his diapers, or lift him in and out of his high chair. I am really struggling with feeling as if I am not able to do anything. I feel pretty useless. My thoughts tell me I can't fulfill my role as mommy; the only thing I can do is fall deeper in love with my boys, which causes even more pain because of the likelihood that I will not be around to watch them grow up.

I mean, y'all, I was a pitiful mess. Things I once had the ability to complete, to perform, or to accomplish no longer existed. Things I loved to do, such as running and exercising, I had no idea if my heart function would ever afford me the ability to do again. Yes, I would eventually be able to lift Hunter from his crib and wrestle with Noah on the floor once the six weeks of postoperative restrictions were lifted. I would even be able to fold a load of laundry using both arms again. As for running, only time would tell. However, those six weeks after having the defibrillator implanted allowed my eyes to see more clearly and my mouth to confess aloud the huge amount of pride and envy I had in my heart. I prided myself on being productive, independent, and functioning at a high capacity. And, yet, here I was forced to ask for help. I know that for some of you reading this, you cannot imagine life without others helping you in some manner or another. For you, asking for help just simply seems like a natural thing to do. For me, I believed that if I needed help with something, then I was failing. Oh, and yes, I have a fear of failure.

The consistency or inconsistency of my journaling was in direct correlation to the amount of time I actually spent reading the Bible. The days and weeks when my Bible went unopened meant that I was not consistently clinging to God's Truth and His Promises. Thus, the lies I believed in my mind spoke louder than God's Word, keeping me blindfolded in the depths of the dark wilderness. If John could coin a term for this period in my life, he would call this "Julie's 'what-if' season." And it was. I truthfully spent more time dwelling on the dooming "what-if" scenarios than on believing God knows best. Romans 8:28

states, "We know that all things work together for the good of those who love God: those who are called according to His purpose," and Romans 8:18 states, "For I consider that the sufferings of this present time are not worth comparing with the glory that is going to be revealed to us." I found that I kept asking myself, *Do I fully believe these two verses in Romans to be true in each and every circumstance? Would these verses not only hold true for the circumstances I am currently facing but also for all scenarios I may potentially face in the future?* At the end of the day, the answer I spoke to my heart was simply, *I have to believe.* I have to believe God's Word is Truth. I have to believe God loves me, and He cares for my soul. I have to believe He is always trustworthy. And, if He is trustworthy, then I can endure any circumstance with hope.

Despite the darkness, despite my self-pity, despite my isolation, despite my own flesh, God was near. He was and is always near because I belong to Him. He was near because of the prayers of friends. He was near because of the Scriptures friends would text me throughout the day, so that regardless of whether or not I had the energy or desire to open the Bible, His Word was pursuing me. My emotions and my feelings cannot keep my Savior from being any less near. And, even in the midst of feeling like I was in an inescapable pit, He began to place within my heart an ability to see things for which I was thankful.

October 28, 2009

Today I feel like I am trying to climb out of a dark hole. I experience moments of complete isolation, sadness, and a desire to be saved. I wish I could go back to the day when

I did not know anything was wrong. It was nice to go through life without fear. Not that I did not fear anything before. It is just that I did not pay attention to my fears. I did not look them in the face every day. I ignored them. Lord, I truly desire to be happy and full of joy again. In the past I did not really have to "work at" being joyful. Right now I do. What am I thankful for? I am thankful for my marriage to John, my children, my Jesus, my church, my parents, my sisters, and my dear friends. I have spent this last week in Dallas while John is traveling. Thank You for my time in Dallas. My childhood home is a safe place for me, a comfort. Thank You for allowing me to spend time with family, with Heather, Linde, Kate, and Grace. Thank You for allowing me to walk the streets I grew up running on! Thank You, thank You that I COULD even JOG! Even though it was only for one minute at a time and slower than many people walk! Mrs. Haley came over to "babysit" me while mom ran a few errands since I still cannot lift the boys. We had a lovely talk about You and treasuring life's moments. Thank You for John's time away in Colorado. Thank you for revealing Yourself to him. I pray that we will live a simple life full of serving, loving one another and others with selflessness. I pray that our children will grow up trusting that You alone are enough to get us through the hardest times. Thank You for the joy my children are to me! Thank You for friends that are serving us as family right now. I continue to pray for healing of my heart and that You will use me as a testimony to others of Your truth, Your holiness, and Your faithfulness.

I ask that You will be the focus of my thoughts—not myself and not self-pity. Allow me to cling to You alone and to *dwell in the presence of the Holy Spirit that surrounds me. Holy Spirit, dwell in my mind, heart, and circumstance. Dwell in our home, within my relationship with John. Make me quick to listen and slow to speak. Make me a vessel of love and understanding. Teach me how to communicate with love and sensitivity in my words rather than keeping things bottled up. I am crying out for help, Lord. I cannot do this life on my own. I have strived with my own strength to climb out of this dark pit for too long, and I continue to fall. I cannot do this life without You.*

> The Lord used three months of wandering in the wilderness to show me Himself in a way that I had not previously known.

The Lord allowed me to experience utter desperation for Him. And He used three months of wandering in the wilderness to show me Himself in a way I had not previously known. Oh, Lord, may I never cease to be desperate for You.

My dearest boys,

I want you to know how faithful the Lord is to pursue after your souls' and hearts' affections. Even in the days, weeks, or months when you feel distant from God, know with certainty that He is near. God's pursuit of our hearts is present whether or not our eyes recognize it, minds acknowledge it, or emotions feel it. There will be seasons in your life when you may have no desire to open your Bible. I pray now for the Lord to raise

up friends who will speak the Truth of the Word into your life
during those times. I pray now for God to raise up an army of
believers who will pray with you and over you in times of need
and in times of plenty. Boys, there is nowhere you can go to
escape the Lord. May you turn to Psalm 139 as I do often to
be reminded of God's all-knowing, ever-present, and endless
pursuing love. I love you!

my heart, mommy

Psalm 139:1–18, 23–24

> LORD, You have searched me and known me.
> You know when I sit down and when I stand up;
> You understand my thoughts from far away.
> You observe my travels and my rest;
> You are aware of all my ways.
> Before a word is on my tongue,
> You know all about it, LORD.
> You have encircled me;
> You have placed Your hand on me.
> This extraordinary knowledge is beyond me.
> It is lofty; I am unable to reach it.
>
> Where can I go to escape Your Spirit?
> Where can I flee from Your presence?
> If I go up to heaven, You are there;
> if I make my bed in Sheol, You are there.
> If I live at the eastern horizon
> or settle at the western limits,

even there Your hand will lead me;
Your right hand will hold on to me.
If I say, "Surely the darkness will hide me,
and the light around me will be night"—
even the darkness is not dark to You.
The night shines like the day;
darkness and light are alike to You.

For it was You who created my inward parts;
You knit me together in my mother's womb.
I will praise You
because I have been remarkably and wonderfully
    made.
Your works are wonderful,
and I know this very well.
My bones were not hidden from You
when I was made in secret,
when I was formed in the depths of the earth.
Your eyes saw me when I was formless;
all my days were written in Your book and
    planned
before a single one of them began.

God, how difficult Your thoughts are
for me to comprehend;
how vast their sum is!
If I counted them,
they would outnumber the grains of sand;
when I wake up, I am still with You.

. . .

Search me, God, and know my heart;
test me and know my concerns.
See if there is any offensive way in me;
lead me in the everlasting way.

Chapter 6

Operation Cover-Up

"But He said to me, 'My grace is sufficient for you, for power is perfected in weakness.'"
2 CORINTHIANS 12:9

As women, most of us have experienced the "ugly cry"—some of us more than others. By "ugly cry" I mean the type of cry that produces such a copious runny nose that not even the softest of tissue can keep the tip of your nose from donning red rawness. And let's just be honest here, these types of cries leave behind evidence of swollen, red eyeballs that even makeup cannot hide.

As I mentioned earlier, the shower was my safe place to have meltdowns. While I never intended to weep crocodile tears each time I stepped into the shower, it just simply turned out that way. I had more cry sessions in those first three months after Hunter was born than in my entire thirty-two years of life combined. Regardless of the tears shed in the confines of a steamy, twenty-square-foot shower, I was bound and determined to accomplish Operation Cover-Up. Too often I attempted to mask the swelling of my red eyeballs by using makeup and throwing on my baseball cap. I had the routine down pat. I would exit our bedroom dressed and ready to greet everyone with a hard-worked, effort-filled smile. I busied myself with the routine tasks of raising two young boys and running a household. And, if that was not enough to fill up my days as it was, I somehow convinced myself that I was ready to start my first job as a pediatric nurse practitioner. I told myself that I did not need to let my education fall by the wayside. After all, I had successfully passed my licensing board exam a few weeks before Hunter's birth. It made complete sense in my brain. Can you just hear my inner dialogue? *It is okay, Julie, you were only diagnosed with heart failure. It's no big deal. Maybe if you begin work and fill your days with more to-do lists, then you can just live as if you were not really given the diagnosis.* All of this made perfect sense in my mind. Denial at its finest. Please tell me I'm not alone here.

Let me just tell you that ignoring the reality around you is not the best strategy for facing tough circumstances. When you fail to take all of the emotions and heartaches and fears of your present circumstances to the Lord, just for the sake of numbing yourself, you are telling God that you believe He messed up and that He did not know what He was doing. This was me. I did this. I was not ready to accept that God actually did *not* mess up by giving me this heart. At the core of ignoring my own reality was my own pride. Pride that said I could write a better story for my life than God could write. Pride that communicated I could decide what is best for my life as I attempted to control my surroundings. My actions demonstrated that I truly didn't believe my God is trustworthy and my source of strength. Sadly I made my best attempt at pulling up my boot straps and moving forward with my own strength and resolve. My mind and my heart were just not ready to process through the circumstances. And so . . . I chose not to.

I am laughing at myself as I pen these words. I mean, y'all, I really did end up sitting down and interviewing with a general pediatrics practice for my first job out of graduate school. This pediatric practice knew me well as I had completed my final semester's clinical rotation with them. Thankfully these two amazing physicians imparted wisdom when I clearly did not have an ounce of good judgment circulating through my brain. These two women compassionately asked me if I was truly ready to embark on a career. Maybe my masked, puffy red eyeballs were a dead giveaway?! They astutely observed my coping mechanism, "If I just keep my mind occupied with other things and focus on caring for other people, I might just be able to ignore and grow numb to my reality." Needless to say, it did not come as a surprise to these two wonderful pediatricians when I phoned them a few days later and confessed to them that they were right. I, indeed, was not ready to head back into the workplace. I could barely keep myself together on the best of days. I mean, even my sweet two-year-old,

At the core of ignoring my own reality was my own pride. Pride that said I could write a better story for my life than God could write.

Noah, noticed that something was a little off with his mommy. Noah often spent a lot of time playing independently, but every once in a while throughout the day, he would come up to me and say, "Hug?" And I would reply, "Of course buddy, Mommy will give you a BIG hug." Noah would then say in his skeptical voice, "Mommy, why you cry?" Hmmm, I wasn't sure what to do with that one so I just hugged him tighter and asked him to go grab a book so I could read to him. If ever there was a time in which I needed Jesus to show up and be my strength, it was now. Because I had none.

> *If ever there was a time in which I needed Jesus to show up and be my strength, it was now. Because I had none.*

November 18, 2009

Lord, I really need You to be my strength. I have too often displayed pride and a sense of self-sufficiency, as if I can do everything on my own. Yet, for the past three months, I have been stripped down of this. I am the weakest I have ever been—physically, emotionally, and spiritually. And, in some strange and crazy way, I do not want that to change. For I am reminded in 2 Corinthians 12:9–10 that when I am weak, God shows up to be powerfully strong through my life, and I want to live a life that is less about my own name and more about Jesus. "But He said to me, 'My grace is sufficient for you, for power is perfected in weakness.' Therefore, I will most gladly boast all the more about my weaknesses, so that Christ's power may reside in me. So I take pleasure in weaknesses, insults, catastrophes, persecutions, and in pressures, because of Christ. For when I am weak, then I am strong."

Unfortunately, I had also chosen to mask the majority of my meltdowns from John. Somehow, even in my weakness, I mustered up enough stubbornness to hide the full truth from him. John was already going through a tough season with work, and I did not want to place even more weight on his shoulders with my burdensome emotions. Sure, John knew I cried from time to time, and he had even witnessed one of those ugly-mess-of-a-cry sessions. But John just thought I was coming off all the pregnancy hormones. It was not until I hit my lowest low that I finally opened up with John to let him into my desperation. In hindsight, I know I should have opened up a lot earlier to John. My silence in our marriage withheld from John the joy of coming alongside me in prayer and speaking the Truth of God's Word over my life. Rather than allowing him to share in the burden and depending on God for grace, I displayed pride in deciding whether or not John was able to carry this burden. When we do not allow our husbands to share in our burdens, we rob them of opportunities to see into our hearts and our hurts. We deprive our husbands of the opportunity to experience God providing for them with all they need to lead us through tough seasons. All because of pride.

November 20, 2009

Lord, I really do praise You for this past weekend. Thank You for giving John and me time in the car to really talk. You gave me the courage to tell him about the dark place I have been sitting in. I think he was in disbelief and honestly a little hurt, okay maybe "little" is an understatement—that I had not shared this with him sooner. In my mind I did not want to burden him. But I realize now that he desires to help carry my burdens. I pray You will protect John, comfort him, fill him with Your grace and Your love. Continually draw his heart to worship You.

"The Stand," by Hillsong United has ministered much to my heart lately. What a gift to be able to sing these words, especially the bridge, with a longing that the lyrics would be true of my life—even in the seasons of suffering. You have given me more days in this life. The realization that You have kept me here on this earth, even when You could have easily brought me home is extremely humbling. And, well, this realization may actually cause me to become even more uncompromising in my convictions, and that's okay. Boldness is actually what You want from my life. Thank You for the gift of a growing perspective, the gift of knowing that life on the earth is fleeting. Lord, thank You for bringing me to a good place today, a place where I desire to laugh rather than cry. It has been a long time since I have laughed without forcing the laughter. Lord, I do not want to miss out on the purpose You have for my life.

I ask that You use this season of my life for Your glory and my good. What I hear from You as I open my Bible and read Your Word today: "Be still and cease striving, Julie. Love your husband that I have given to you. Speak of Me to your children that I have entrusted to you. Share your story that I have given you. Do not be scared to invest in others. And this does not mean only listening and being there for others but sharing your own heart and being vulnerable yourself."

Lord, the cross is real! Your suffering and Your death were painful and beautiful all at the same time. I am so thankful You are revealing to me that something beautiful can come from such a painful season. I am beginning to believe You really will use this current suffering for something greater than I can grasp entirely. Thank You for the life You have given me. I pray that You will remind me daily of the gift it is to be where I am right now.

Sweet boys,

As your mommy, my flesh wants for you to have a life filled with joy, laughter, and many, many successes. Yet, my soul knows that it is in the challenges of this life and in the failures when your character is tested by fire and your true beliefs are revealed. When your weaknesses rise to the surface of life . . . when your weaknesses are brought from the darkness into the light . . . it is there, in the light, where God's grace proves all-sufficient. To fully experience God's abundant grace, we must break down the barriers of silence and our tendency to hide. The gospel of Jesus Christ is our good news. Through Jesus' death and resurrection, our sins have been fully paid for by His blood. Believing that the gospel is enough—that

*there is nothing we can do to earn more of His love or do
anything to lose His love and His grace over our lives——is the
belief that allows us to live freely, transparently, and without
shame. Boys, Jesus covers our imperfections and our faults. We
are made whole through the blood of Jesus spilled upon the
cross and His glorious resurrection. He defeated the grave so
that we, too, might say to death, "Death, where is your sting?"
(1 Cor. 15:55). So my prayer over your lives is that you will be
aware of and recognize your weaknesses. And, thus, cling to
God's fulfilling grace.*

I love you . . . my heart, mommy

Chapter 7

Glimpses of Light

"*The* LORD *is my rock, my fortress,
and my deliverer, my God, my mountain
where I seek refuge, my shield and the horn
of my salvation, my stronghold.*"
PSALM 18:2

The Lord was so gracious and faithful to give me glimpses of His light in such a season of darkness. Slowly over time I found that the dark days were not quite as dark as they were the weeks and months before. In fact, I began to find joy in adjusting to my "new normal." By the time Thanksgiving came around, the tears that fell down my cheeks transitioned from tears rooted in fear into tears of gratefulness to face another day.

I continued battling the fearful thoughts. Thoughts of kissing John good-bye in the morning and not knowing if it would be our last morning routine. Thoughts of collapsing while pushing the boys in the stroller as we went out for morning walks. Thoughts of wondering if I would even wake up in the morning as I lay my head down on my pillow at night. Throughout this journey, there were moments when the thoughts would win. But I have some people, "my people" in this life, and my people would not let me forget the Word of God. There would be weeks when I would not open my Bible because I was too sad, and frankly, I wanted to stay sad. Then I would check my e-mail, open a card, or read a text message on my phone from friends who would share what Scriptures they were praying over me and boom . . . Truth would enter my mind. When I did not want to pursue Jesus, He was relentless in pursuing after me.

Friends from every season of our lives continued to send words of encouragement and lists of ways they were praying. Let me just take a moment to implore you: please do not be the friend who solely prays in the midst of crisis and the season of chaos. Rather, be the friend that perseveres in prayer and encouragement. As time passes, be the friend that reaches out to know the needs of those around you. Even in the adjustment to a new normal, continue to faithfully pray and be available. Because there will still be days when the darkness hovers. Out of the blue, when you think all is better, your friend, coworker, neighbor might just be slipping back into believing the voices of the world and need Truth spoken into her mind, her

> *Be the friend that perseveres in prayer and encouragement.*

heart, her life. Listen to that voice in your stomach or your heart, and pick up the phone or send an e-mail or, for goodness' sake, drive over unannounced. Just because. I promise you will be used by Jesus.

Yes, the truth of God's Word began to replace my fearful thoughts. This does not mean the fears disappeared altogether because they certainly did not. Rather, I began to have a weapon with which to fight against the fears. And I began slowly to open up with those friends that were in our tight community, with those who were that "safe place" to be vulnerable. But as for that larger circle of friends, I still held on to that masked smile.

If you live in the South, you know what I mean when I say that it was time to pull together the annual Christmas card photo. And, if you do not live in the South, allow me to let you in on a little secret. There is a real and unspoken pressure to produce a really great family Christmas card. It can be a considerable undertaking because of all that goes into the creation of the card itself and actually sending them to people. The photo shoot alone can be overwhelming! You schedule the shoot with the photographer and hope your children will be willing and joyful participants. That is, after you have bribed them—ahem, I mean convinced them to be happy about wearing the perfectly coordinated outfits you spent days searching for as if going on a citywide scavenger hunt. Don't think I haven't contemplated allowing the kids to dress in a random assortment of superhero costumes just for fun. Maybe this year?! And do I dare mention keeping an up-to-date list of friends' addresses? The list could go on and on.

When it comes to sending the annual Christmas card, people generally fall into one of three categories. First are those who drop their Christmas cards in the mail so others receive it no later than the first of December. The second category are the people whose Christmas cards get pushed down the priority list and thus turn into New Year's cards or maybe Groundhog Day cards. Over the last couple of years, there has been a growing constituency of bold rebels (just kidding!), those who simply bypass the entire Christmas card altogether. Sometimes I wonder if this third group is actually the smartest of the bunch as they do not succumb to the pressure of mailing out a card, and yet they get to sit back and simply enjoy all the cards that flood into their mailbox.

On this particular year I was not convinced that we would send out a New Year's card, let alone a Christmas card. I persuaded myself it would simply be easier not to send a card. In fact, I guarantee everyone would've understood given our circumstances. I mean, postoperative restrictions were imposed on my life until the week before Thanksgiving. However, John surprised me one night at dinner when he leaned over and said, "Julie, I think you should write a letter to put in our Christmas card this year." *Enter awkward silence.* Well, OF COURSE! Of course we should take a family photo that portrays that life is all hunky-dory. Of course, I should spill my heart out on paper for all to see. Umm, No! No. Thank. You. And, just in case you were wondering, no. I did not speak aloud the opinionated thoughts that were going through my mind in that moment. Rather I just stared down at the food on my plate. My mind was racing. Should I just ignore his suggestion? Should I quickly come up with some excuse to shoot his whole idea down? Should I step away from the table because "I'm pretty sure I hear" our littlest one crying from his crib? Should I ask John if he needs more to eat? But, as the silence grew almost deafening, I somehow responded with an extremely hesitant and almost inaudible *okay*.

Oh, how I did not want to write that letter. Writing the letter was going to force me to step away from my nice, cozy, and warm place of comfort and safety. After all, I was only, just then, becoming comfortable with letting John in on all I was processing. All fronts of my life were being rocked—physically, emotionally, and spiritually. Yet somehow John was now asking me to enlarge the reach of my vulnerability.

Each day, while the boys were taking their naps, I would sit down in front of my computer and make my best attempt at writing *"the"* Christmas letter. After two weeks— yes, TWO weeks—I reached the end product. Because I didn't want the letter to be too heavy, I had worked hard to incorporate cleverly articulated and humorous banter between medical updates. I was convinced John would be pleased. In fact, I had envisioned the approval I would receive from him after he completed a once-over of the letter. As I said before, John is by far the better storyteller between the two of us. Too often I leave out most of the descriptive details and jump straight to the end of the story. However, this time was different. The Christmas letter. I mean, wow, in *my* opinion, this was some good material!

Well, the time had come for me to share the letter with John. I was a little nervous—the happy kind of nervous. I slowly walked over to the sofa and snuggled close to John. I softly asked, "Would you like to read through the letter I have been working on?" John, somewhat torn between the football game playing on the television and the nervous excitement displayed on my face, nodded to accept the challenge. I opened up the laptop and leaned over and gave him a quick kiss on the cheek. "Thank you for loving me more than the Vikings" (John's favorite NFL team).

John began to read paragraph after paragraph with me leaning over onto his shoulder so that I could read along with him. I smiled and silently laughed as I read through all of the *funny* comments. As John came to the end, he slowly and gently closed the laptop. Without even turning to make eye contact, he said, "Julie, I love you. Honestly? It's awful." What?! Awful? It was due to go to print in the morning!

"You are joking, right?" I responded with a smidge of defensiveness. Okay, maybe a bit more than a smidge.

With the sweetest, most gentle tone in his voice, John looked at me and said, "Julie, it is terrible." At this point I punched my linebacker husband in the shoulder as hard as I could. Seriously. I did. I punched him. I am not proud of it. Hitting him in the shoulder was definitely not a wise response on my part. I did apologize later that evening. But in that moment I simply could not find the words to respond. Thus, John's deltoid muscle was the recipient of my pent-up, accumulating anger from the preceding three months of tough circumstances.

Once John discerned that I had calmed down, he patiently said that after all we'd been through, the last thing he expected was for me to minimize the emotions through *poor* use of humor. Deep down, I knew he was right. My eyeballs became wet, and I believe a few tears fell down my cheeks. Go figure, right? But did I really want to be that vulnerable? Did I really want to share my heart and all the fears I was processing? My pride wanted to be right, to win the discussion, and send out the lighthearted, not-so-clever letter. However, my soul knew I was wrong. And I needed to listen to my soul and my husband instead of my pride.

I scooted to the far end of the sofa. I reopened the laptop, opened up a blank document, and began to type. It took me less than seventeen minutes to bare my heart. I was a blubbering mess. My fingers were unable to keep up with the words flowing from my heart. And this time, as John scrolled through the newly written letter, he said with tears in his own eyes, "This is it. This is what our friends are going to want to know. This describes what Jesus has been doing in your heart."

He was right. It turns out that our friends desired vulnerability from us, not a covered-up, stoic, and "all is fine and dandy" letter. In the weeks following Christmas, many made phone calls and sent messages responding with words of encouragement and ways in which they were covering us in prayer. Some even courageously shared the

When we take the first step in vulnerability, it allows us the opportunity to be a safe place for others to take the courageous step to be vulnerable, too.

reality behind their own family photos. John and I, then, were given opportunities to pray for friends in specific ways after they opened their hearts to us. You know, it is amazing what happens when we take the first step in vulnerability. It allows us the opportunity to be a safe place for others to take the courageous step to be vulnerable, too.

Yes, the risk of vulnerability can be scary. It is true that the Holy Spirit often leads us into areas where we feel vulnerable. But we can go there because, in God, we have eternal security. Though it feels "dangerous" to walk in this direction, we are already safe in the embrace of God's powerful love—so no place is truly dangerous for us. And, when the Holy Spirit leads us to be vulnerable, God shows up and blesses us through it with His peace and freedom.

Boys,

Let me talk with you about risk as it pertains to faith in Jesus. Living a life for the Lord is going to be risky. You may observe a classmate really struggling, and you will take the risk to ask him if you can pray with him. You may have the opportunity on the ball field to choose to use words that build up and not words that tear down your teammates or your opponents. You may have a conversation with a friend and sense the Holy Spirit wants you to share the story of how Jesus pursued your soul. You may one day sell off your belongings here in the United States and move across the world to share the gospel with people who have never heard the name of Jesus, or maybe you will financially support friends that do. All of these things can be scary if you are focusing on yourself. But, if you focus on God's promise that He is always with you, never leaves you, and is always working things for your good and for His glory, then risk taking can actually bring your heart much joy. See, we can take steps of faith without being consumed with fear. And even when fear creeps into your mind and emotions, you can continue stepping forward into that situation, trusting in the Lord to be all you need. Because He is just that . . . He is all we need. Through the risks you take for Jesus, He will use you in the lives of others. Through risking for Jesus, your life will display that you value the Lord more than stuff, more than accolades, more than the things of the world that fade. I am praying for Jesus to make you risk takers for the gospel . . . risk takers for vulnerability . . . risk takers in sharing God's promises.

I love you!

my heart, mommy

Chapter 8

Numbered Days

*"Man's days are determined and the number
of his months depends on You, and . . .
You have set limits he cannot pass."*
JOB 14:5

As the months progressed, my physical heart did not improve much. My spiritual heart, on the other hand, had grown to accept and embrace my physical circumstances as a gift from the Lord that He was using to give me an eternal perspective through which to view this life. Instead of focusing on the things I was losing or even what I *might* lose, the Lord was gently focusing my eyes on the gifts He was giving me day by day. And His Word, written in Lamentations 3:22–23, stating His mercies are new every morning proved true. As for my physical health, John and I were grateful to the Lord that my heart function had not worsened. This meant, for the time being, we could take a deep breath knowing that I would not need to be placed on the heart-transplant waiting list. Additionally, despite the fluttering and racing heartbeats, my ICD had not needed to shock my heart since my time in the hospital. This was just one more thing for which to be thankful. Even in the hard days when my shortness of breath and light-headedness were more pronounced, the Lord consistently gave us grateful hearts for the littlest, often disguised blessings in our days as a family.

The Lord was also teaching me to trust that He is indeed trustworthy no matter the circumstance. He was extending me the faith to believe I could trust Him and His Word. The doctors would often refer to the ICD as my reliable "insurance policy." Because of the device's ability to immediately recognize when my heart rhythm needs to be regulated, the ICD would likely help extend my life. For many these words shared from the mouths of doctors would bring comfort or security, but my hope is not found in the words of my physicians. Rather my ultimate hope is found in the words of my Father in heaven who actually created every muscle fiber and electrical pathway in my heart.

In Job 14:5, Job speaks to God saying, "Man's days are determined and the number of his months depends on You, and . . . You have set limits he cannot pass." Job was aware that a man's days are numbered. This verse means the moment each one of us will meet our Maker is already written by the Lord. No failure of my heart is outside of His hand. The ICD cannot sustain me one second longer than He intends for me to live, and my irregular heartbeat cannot take me home a minute before He is ready for me to be there. My faith does not rest in electrical currents and the pumping of my heart muscle. Rather my faith is set on the Creator of the universe who rules over all things, including my death. Yes, our God has set limits on our lives that we cannot outlive or preemptively shorten outside of His sovereign, all-powerful hand. I believe He has numbered my days. With or without the ICD implanted in the left side of my chest, I cannot change or alter His established time line for my life this side of heaven.

> *The moment each one of us will meet our Maker is already written by the Lord.*

This growing faith, which can only be accredited to Jesus, allows me to enjoy each day for the day itself. Simply put, I began to live with joy again. Instead of focusing on the unknown and wondering when Jesus would call me home, my focus turned toward intentionally living each day I was given. I started experiencing freedom from my fears. Not because my fears somehow disappeared, but rather my trust and faith in God, who actually loves and cares for me and has the power to tell the waves where to stop on the shore and calm the sea with the sound of His voice, is the bigger driving force in my life. I rest not in the power of my fears but in the power of my God.

Nearly one year later I had the opportunity to share of the Lord's grace and mercy over my physical heart and my soul with a group of women at our church. Some of the women in the room had been with John and me from day one of this journey, while others were unaware of what the last year of our family's life had entailed. As I sat on a metal stool in the front of the classroom, I read the revised version of the Christmas letter. The emotions were still as raw as they were the evening the words flew out of my heart and onto the computer screen. I could feel my body warring between mind and soul and reliving the real fight to believe Truth and not my fears. And somehow at the exact same time, sharing with these ladies brought me so much joy. It brought me joy to share of the nearness of my Savior. Yes, there was even joy in recounting the season of darkness. Even now, speaking of how God's Truth pulled me out of the darkness allows me to remember how amazing the nearness of Jesus and His love truly is. In the dark pit of fear, Jesus found me and pursued after my soul to worship Him in deeper and more sincere ways. The Lord Almighty was then and is now worthy of all the praise and glory for what He has done and is doing in my life.

After bearing my heart that Sunday morning, the class was dismissed. The remaining fifteen minutes of our class time were undeniably emotional and heavy. In fact, most people were not in a rush to leave even though I exceeded the allotted time frame. In typical girl fashion, several of my friends greeted me with hugs as I made it back over to my belongings, and they affirmed me in my vulnerability. After a few minutes of visiting, we exited the quieted classroom to find ourselves filtering into the crowd of people arriving for the worship service. As my friends stopped to mingle, I continued on rather than pausing for hugs and hellos with friends as is typical for me. Somewhere between leaving the classroom and entering the mezzanine of the building, it was evident that something was not right inside my body.

All of my energy was focused on physically making it to the nursery to pick up Noah and Hunter. As I walked, the pressure in my chest and neck intensified. With each step breathing became more difficult. My face increasingly felt warm and sweaty. Once I finally reached Noah's classroom, I placed the majority of my upper body weight on the half door to the classroom. I forced a smile on my already tensed face when I saw Noah's eyes meet mine. He threw the toys he was playing with to the side and ran straight over to the doorway. I was able to say "thank you" to the nursery volunteers, but I did not linger long enough to hear how he did in the classroom. Noah took hold of my right hand and walked steadily next to my leg as we turned the corner to walk down the adjacent hallway to find Hunter's classroom. Now I cannot say with certainty that Noah sensed something was wrong. But I will say that for his barely three-year-old "run as fast as you can at all times" self, it was the first time ever—I mean EVER—that I didn't need to remind him to stay with me rather than dart away in the opposite direction.

By the time we reached Hunter's classroom, my vision and hearing had become clouded, and I struggled to take a deep breath. It felt as if all the blood returning to my heart from all over my body was getting trapped in my neck. I asked one of the volunteers in Hunter's classroom if she could help me get the boys to the car because I was quickly losing all energy. How I thought I would be able to drive them home is beyond me. When I could not finish my signature in order to sign out Hunter, I calmly and authoritatively spoke to the volunteers, "I am going to collapse." I pointed to one volunteer, "You need to call 9-1-1." I turned to another volunteer and said, "Please call my husband, John Manning. His number is in my phone. Call 9-1-1 first!" And, I collapsed to the ground.

In front of my two children and twenty plus other toddlers, I collapsed to the ground. I heard the cries of my own two precious boys as well as the other children as I lay there on the cold, concrete floor. What I had feared most, becoming lifeless on the floor in front of my children, was happening. All I could think was, *This is it. This is my time.* I lay there with increasing pressure in my chest and foggy thoughts. With my eyes closed, all I could do was thank Jesus for giving me fifteen months with my boys. He allowed me to watch Noah grow to love reading books and complete puzzles. Jesus allowed me to watch Hunter learn how to walk and hear him call me "Mamma." The end had never felt so near.

> *All I could think was, **This is it. This is my time.***

A wonderful, kind man at our church, who is also a physician, quickly came into the nursery room as one of the volunteers was on the phone with the 9-1-1 operator. With my eyes still closed, I overheard him say, "Her pulse is weak. I am only counting thirty beats per minute." I do not know when two of my sweet friends rushed in, but at some point I heard Jen and Kimberly praying over me. Their hands were firmly placed on my right hip and right shoulder. I opened my eyes and weakly said, "I need you to tell my boys about Jesus. Please. Please. You have to tell my boys about Jesus because I am not going to be here to tell them." And I shut my eyes.

Boys,

With tears in my eyes, I write you this letter. I spent many months fearing that I would collapse in front of you. I feared that this would scare you so terribly and negatively impact your sweet hearts. All I wanted and still want to do as your mommy is protect you from the image of Mommy falling to the floor and not waking up. Yet this fear of mine actually did happen. My fear became reality, and unfortunately, I have collapsed several times in front of you over the past six years. In this life, when the things you and I fear do happen . . . because some of them will happen . . . God's grace, His mercy, and His love are sufficient to meet our every need in those moments. My heart prays that your minds will not dwell on your fear, but rather on the One who will strengthen you to overcome those fears and endure you through those circumstances if and when they come to pass. May you live this life not delegating power to your fears but resting in the knowledge and truth that power rightfully and solely belongs to the Lord . . . and to Him alone! I love you boys with all of my heart.

my heart, mommy

Chapter 9

This Life Is Not My Own

"For me, living is Christ and dying is gain."
PHILIPPIANS 1:21

No consuming brightness this time . . . just waiting for what I anticipated would be my body surrendering to its end. But minutes later, EMS arrived. My body felt increasingly weak, and I was not much help in recounting all that had taken place. Thankfully, the church nursery volunteers and friends were able to give the paramedic team a recap of the preceding events. As the paramedics got to work, one of the team members started an IV in my right arm, and another placed stickers and wires on my chest that would connect to the cardiac monitor. I was then given a dissolvable pill under my tongue, which they hoped would relieve some of the pressure in my chest. Even after a few minutes the pressure in my neck and chest persisted. I felt like my neck was filling up like a water balloon to the point where the balloon would succumb to the pressure and burst.

The paramedic then gave me a second dose of the same pill under my tongue as they were loading me onto the stretcher. For a moment I thought I was hallucinating when I heard John's voice as they were tightening the straps across my legs and abdomen to secure me to the stretcher. I knew John was at our church's other location all the way across town. Surely there was no way he could have raced back over so quickly. But as I forced open my eyes, there he stood. Tears in his eyes, but with a smile on his face. My Johnny.

The paramedic team loaded me into the ambulance, which is never a gentle or comfortable experience. As the sirens started blaring, the paramedic asked me once again if I felt any relief of the pressure in my chest. And, once more, I whispered painfully, "No. It is really bad." Despite my blood pressure being low, she placed a patch, this time, of the same medicine on my left chest. Finally, within two or three minutes, the pressure began to slowly lift. With much relief I no longer felt as if my neck and chest were going to explode.

I suffered a heart attack that morning. Even the emergency-room (ER) physician was hesitant to say the diagnosis until my second set of blood work came back exclaiming without a shadow of doubt that my heart muscle had taken a hit, had endured more damage, had suffered from a period of time where oxygen was not properly delivered to my heart's muscle.

Looking back, the Lord was extremely gracious to have allowed the heart attack to happen when it did and where it did. He allowed me to be surrounded by friends that love my family. He allowed me to experience being prayed over within seconds of collapsing. I was not driving my children home from church by myself, which had I not delayed leaving our classroom that morning, may well have been the case. I was not alone at home without a cell phone close to me. Yes, my boys witnessed Mommy falling to the ground, but they had sweet friends of ours who immediately removed them from the room, kept them entertained, kept their bellies full, and reassured them that Jesus was watching over Mommy and loved them very much. Yes, Jesus displayed such grace upon our family that Sunday morning.

I was admitted as an inpatient that afternoon, knowing that I would need to have an exploratory heart surgery performed the next

> *This life is not my own to control. I can only surrender to the One who has authored my days.*

day. John and I spent the rest of the afternoon praising the Lord for His nearness over our boys and us and for His grace over our lives. Once again I felt the weight of the reality that this life is not my own to control, but rather I can only surrender to the One who has authored my days.

The following morning I was once again wheeled into an operating room. After being asked by one of the OR staff if I would like to listen to any particular music while we waited on the anesthesiologist to arrive, I requested music by Chris Tomlin. I had no idea how the people in the room would respond to this request, but I did not give it much thought honestly. All I knew was that I wanted to fall asleep worshipping the Lord. There on the cold, hard surface of the operating table, my ears recognized the first song that came across the speaker from the corner of the room. It was "Amazing Grace." It was the only song I would hear in the operating room that day. And, let me tell you, there is nothing more calming to the soul than falling asleep proclaiming the amazing grace of our Savior Jesus. He displayed such grace over the previous day's circumstances, and then in that moment my heart could not help but worship the Lord for the amazing grace He poured out to save my soul and offer me life eternal with Him . . . forever.

As I drifted off, I prayed, "Lord, if You are willing, You will awaken me from yet again another surgery, but if not, I know I will awaken to see You. You, Lord, have my heart. Help me believe what Paul wrote is true: to live is Christ, and to die is gain."

The Lord was already answering that prayer. He had been answering that prayer over the past year as I processed the fragility of my own life, and the Holy Spirit started challenging me as I asked myself, *What am I really living for?* The world would say that fighting to live so my children can grow up with a mommy is a noble and loving cause. And, yes, it is. I cannot deny that. The world would say contributing to and serving our local community is also noble and legacy leaving. And, yes, it is. But all of this is rubbish if people's souls, my children's souls, do not feel the love of Jesus through my life or hear His name proclaimed from my lips.

Addressing the Philippian believers Paul writes from prison (Phil. 1:12–14): "Now I want you to know, brothers, that what has happened to me has actually resulted in the advance of the gospel, so that it has become known throughout the whole imperial guard, and to everyone else, that my imprisonment is in the cause of Christ. Most of the brothers in the Lord have gained confidence from my imprisonment and dare even more to speak the message fearlessly."

The message of Christ was not contained, not hindered, not restricted through Paul's imprisonment. In fact, it was the opposite. The gospel was spread throughout the entire imperial guard. It is hard to believe that this would have happened without Paul's conviction to be bold within the walls of the prison. Additionally, other believers grew in confidence to share Christ with boldness and not timidity. I meditated on these verses for weeks as I asked God to show me how my own circumstances of living with heart disease and living with the risk of a sudden cardiac death could be used for the furthering of the gospel.

At this point, God obviously was not ready for my faith to become sight. After all, He has had multiple opportunities to snatch me up. But, rather, He chose to breathe life back into my body twice and awaken me from three heart surgeries. So I begged God to show me through His Word what He has purposed for my life. I was not longing for some larger-than-life task. I'm still not. I found that I did not need to do much more than raise my eyes from my bowed head to see a couple pairs of eyeballs staring at me, asking to build a tent out of sheets in the living room. With fresh eyes I noticed families that awaited me behind clinic-room doorways and hospital-room curtains as souls that needed to be loved and cared for with empathy and a servant's heart. I began to see that everyday living, mundane errands and laundry, really was and is for Jesus, for sharing Him and experiencing Him this side of heaven. So others might come to know His love, His grace, His mercy, and His salvation. I desire to live moment to moment for Jesus with intentionality, not just in public but behind closed doors when no one is watching.

Paul continues in Philippians 1:20–21: "My eager expectation and hope is that I will not be ashamed about anything, but that now as always, with all boldness, Christ will be highly honored in my body, whether by life or by death. For me, living is Christ and dying is gain."

For me to repeat aloud verse 21 now, it does not only sound good in theory or simply sound good for Paul, but this verse is now a checkpoint for my heart. Am I really living for Jesus in this very moment? Am I living for Jesus in my tasks? In my to-do lists? In my rest? In my time behind the wheel driving my kids to their team practices and games? And the answer always seems to come back to this question: Am I being intentional with the time Jesus has given me? Am I being purposeful with the moments God is allowing me to breathe and my heart to beat? So, yes, Lord, to go on living here on the earth better be for You because if it isn't, then You should go ahead and bring me home . . . because You are better.

My heart, my mind, and my soul get it. Not by my own wisdom or understanding, but through experiencing Jesus' nearness in my life. Yes, I yearn desperately to be back surrounded by brightness and the presence of the Lord. I really do. I long for the day when my soul is no longer wrestling inside of me, battling the tension between wanting to reach our fiftieth wedding anniversary, wanting to watch our boys grow into men, and desiring the most amazing Truth of beholding the Lamb and witnessing the saints in heaven worshipping the God of the universe as He rightly sits on the throne of grace.

But until that day comes . . . when the tension is gone, I pray that Jesus will direct my eyes and focus my thoughts on being fully present in the moment I have been given and with whom it has been given. I do not want to waste the breaths He is giving me, for He may just call me home tonight. Yet, as I await the moment when the unseen becomes visible, may I live and breathe Jesus here on this earth, following Him with joy and obedience, knowing that this place is not home. One day . . . I will be home.

> *As I await the moment when the unseen becomes visible, may I live and breathe Jesus here on this earth, following Him with joy and obedience, knowing that this place is not home.*

My Boys,

This is truly my prayer over your lives: I pray that as you grow into young men, you will reflect a heart of surrender. Surrendering to Jesus takes courage, and it produces the fruit of both humility and wisdom. As you surrender to the ways of the Lord, I pray your life will reflect the light of Christ. Through surrender you lay down those things that are not life-giving for those things that satisfy the soul. As Jesus said to the Samaritan woman at the well in John 4:13–14, "Everyone who drinks from this water will get thirsty again. But whoever drinks from the water that I will give him will never get thirsty again—ever! In fact, the water I will give him will become a well of water springing up within him for eternal life." May your eyes be quick to recognize when you are drinking things that will leave you thirsty, and may your heart turn to what will forever quench your thirst—Jesus. Please know that surrendering is not a "one and done" event. Rather, as long as you are living on this earth where our flesh and our soul battle with one another, surrendering areas of your life will be a daily decision. Whether it's your fears or those things you love or trust more than Jesus—such as, your time, being in control, or objects of comfort—you will have daily choices to make. Boys, this place, this earth is not your home. But each one of you has been given the opportunity to live this life with intentionality in everything you say and do. God desires to use your lives this side of heaven for His purposes, and in His time He will bring you home to be with Him. This is joy. I pray this is joy for you, too.

I love you . . . more and more every day.

my heart, mommy

Chapter 10

Taking a Risk

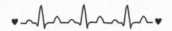

*"Now we have this treasure in clay jars, so that this
extraordinary power may be from God and not from us."*
2 CORINTHIANS 4:7

When I wrote that Christmas letter on our couch, I never
expected to find myself taking a much larger risk in writing the pages of this book. Writing books is reserved for
more well-known people. Writing books is reserved for
more influential people, reserved for those with social
media platforms. Not me, a part-time working mother of
three. (Wait, three? Yes, three. You will hear more about
the gift of our youngest son in a little while.) But, honestly,
I sit here laughing at myself when I look at all the things *I*
have viewed as risk. What I have viewed as *risk*, Jesus
views as obedience. The Lord has simply asked me to trust
Him as I take one step of faith at a time. And I kind of
wonder what would happen if each one of us would fall on

our faces in prayer and consistently read and meditate on the Word of God. I mean, really . . . what would happen if we would just take the time and quiet our lives down long enough to sense the Holy Spirit directing our steps in places our logical, worldly minds would likely never take us? I am praying right now for you as you read this book. *Lord Jesus, will You move Your daughter to embrace living a life of risk as she takes one step at a time in faith. Jesus, will You place within our hearts a sense of urgency to live a life that demonstrates and declares Your gospel.*

*What I have viewed as **risk**, Jesus views as obedience.*

Your steps of faith may not seem monumental to you. Or maybe they will. Maybe they will actually feel monumental. I don't know. However, what I do know is that God has a purpose for your life. And that purpose is for you to have a surrendered heart, allowing God to use your life to display Jesus. The Lord desires to be declared and demonstrated within what we categorize as mundane as well as in what we categorize as extraordinary. He wants the glory when a mom sorts and folds laundry and cleans toilets for the thousandth time just as much as He does when a mom finds herself on the other side of the world sharing the gospel with an unreached people group. He desires a heart of faith from the woman that steps into a beginner Bible study in her neighborhood as much as He does from the woman that stands in front of a crowd of one thousand to teach His Word. God wants to be the focus of the mother's mind as she reads *Good Night Moon* every night to her growing baby just as He wants to be the focus of the woman's mind that is studying for medical school or law school exams. Yes, God desires to use your life and my life to shine His light, speak His truth, be His hands, and display His love, compassion, and mercy.

For me, when I slowed down, sat down, stopped talking, and actually allowed God's Word to soak into my heart and my mind, I actually sensed the Holy Spirit. He moved me toward openness, humility, and vulnerability and away from pride, self-reliance, productivity, and control. You may think I immediately jumped into obediently walking in faith in every single one of these areas. But you would be wrong. I didn't. I tiptoed a little, but I did not do a cannonball off the diving board. Sadly, what I believed God was asking of me and from me, I kept silent. I did not share it with anyone initially. Yet as days and weeks passed, I could not shake it. I could not run away from it. I could not even suppress it. The Holy Spirit kept convicting my heart day after day. I kept telling Him, *Surely not me, Lord. Surely, not me. You can accomplish Your work through the well known. You don't need everyday me to speak up.* But that is the thing about God. He uses the underdog. He uses the ordinary. He uses the simple. He uses the humble. He uses the sinner. He uses the ones that feel underqualified. He uses those that simply realize they need Him. And God is faithful to pursue His children until they can no longer ignore, push away, or resist His hand on their lives.

On New Year's Eve 2012, John and I had plans to spend time with two other couples who are some of our closest friends. Because we are superfun people—we really are fun, seriously—the six of us decided to go see a movie. Yes, a movie. Please, do not count us out yet! It was, after all, an iMAX movie! And, in fact, we were going to push our limits and do our best to stay awake until midnight, an hour I had not seen since working the night shift at the hospital. As for our strategy, you might ask? We convinced ourselves we could locate some yummy dessert and caffeinated coffee to fuel our quest to ring in the New Year Central Standard Time.

As we were leaving the movie theater, we drove past a well-known bakery in town and noticed that not only were the lights on, but the place was a packed house. We snatched up one of the last few available parking spaces and boisterously walked through the parking lot up to the front door. We swung open the glass-paneled door with nearly every head at every table turning to look at what the wind had blown in through the front entrance. It did not take us but maybe two seconds to realize that we had crashed an invitation-only, black-tie dinner event. We later learned that the invitation list consisted of only family, friends, and those who had financially invested in the bakery. Oops!

We attempted to backpedal as we apologized for interrupting their evening. But one of our husbands, who will rename nameless—ahem, John—somehow convinced one of the waiters to let us join the party. John has never been bothered by awkwardness. John, with a huge grin on his face, boldly asked one of the waiters if it would be too much trouble for us to just grab coffee and dessert at the counter "to go." As the waiter went to ask the manager, we uncomfortably and somewhat embarrassingly huddled by the front door as if we were jam-packed in a tiny elevator. When the waiter returned, he smiled and welcomed us into the restaurant. Without trying to cause more of a scene than we already had, the six of us slowly made our way to the coffee counter without a peep from our mouths. The owner, Russell, a jolly old fellow donning his own Happy New Year's hat, came over and introduced himself to John. Their conversation quickly escalated from a simple handshake to the exchange of hugs and high-fives. Well, of course it did?! Before we knew it, our heads were adorned with "2012" tiaras and "Happy New Year" headbands.

Russell hosts this appreciation dinner every year for the restaurant's investors, and they celebrate the New Year at 10:00 p.m. Did I mention we walked in at 9:52 p.m.?! The restaurant was full of smiles and lively conversations. And the six of us were giggling so hard at what we were experiencing that our eyes began to well up with tears. Well, maybe not our husbands, but Jennie, Bekah, and I were hysterically laughing. Russell raised his glass as he grabbed hold of the microphone. The restaurant grew politely quiet as Russell began his emotional toast. "Most of all, I want to thank Mom and Dad, and all of you investors who believed in this project." Like the climax of a beautiful symphony, Russell's voice grew with passion and veracity, as he joyfully shouted, "And, to [awkward pause] John, [awkward pause] John and his friends," and then just tears. Sweet Russell took a handkerchief from his pocket and wiped his tears. "To our new FRIENDS!" Yes, Russell, to your new friends that interrupted your lovely, black-tie, invitation-only dinner party. We were instantly welcomed into the Russell family. We gave hugs to strangers that night as we grabbed our coffees and our red velvet cake pristinely packaged in a white bakery box adorned with a bow.

We laughed all the way back to our cars in the crowded parking lot, amused as we rhetorically asked one another, "What in the world just happened?!"

We continued our evening enjoying coffee and cake back at our home. It was a crisp, chilly evening, but that did not deter us from gathering outside on our deck overlooking the downtown Austin skyline. The sky was even clear enough to see the stars hanging above our heads. Our hysterical laughter calmed to chuckles as we recounted our experience at the bakery, and we slowly transitioned into the type of conversation we do best—deep. In true Zac fashion, he posed a question for our group: "How has God shown His faithfulness over your life in 2011, and what might He be asking of you in 2012?"

Under what felt like the weight of a ton of bricks, my heart fell directly into my belly. Okay, so not literally. But, I did feel the weight of the Holy Spirit's conviction as I immediately knew the answer to the questions posed. After all, for the last few months I had kept the prompting under lock and key. However, I gladly embraced the silence that followed, allowing others to begin sharing. Brandon was the first, then Bekah. As the minutes passed, the palms of my hands grew sweaty, and my heart began beating faster and faster, *Lord, really? I will gladly speak of Your faithfulness; any day, every time, I will speak of the many ways You have proved Yourself faithful. But do I really have to speak of what You might ask of me this coming year? Can I not just hold onto this for a little while longer?* But I knew deep down that the only way to stop my heart from racing was to be vulnerable with those I trusted most and loved deeply.

John turned his eyes toward me as Bekah finished sharing her answers. Jennie, who was sitting to my right, then said, "Well, Julie, what about you?" *Oh, okay, Lord, no more procrastinating.* I took in a deep breath, let out a small sigh, and proceeded to share the ways I saw God's faithfulness over my life. Then, I confessed my fear in voicing what I was about to speak aloud for the first time. While I spoke with passion and courage as I shared of God's faithfulness, my tone changed in answering the latter question. I began the sentence staring at the ground right in front of me. "I think I am supposed to"—I raised my head to look into John's eyes, and then I slowly turned toward Jennie, "I think I am supposed to share my story." As quickly as it was said, I wanted to retract it back into my mouth. But I couldn't. It was out there. It was out there for those whom I love and those who love me. For them to walk alongside me in whatever avenues the Lord would have me share.

In hindsight, I was nervous to say aloud what I believed God was asking of me because, what if I was wrong?! I didn't want to be wrong. I did not want to open myself up for failure. I had conversations in my head asking the question, *What if my emotions were conjuring up the answer and not the Holy Spirit?* This is just plain nonsense. God wants us to talk about Him and how He has shown up in our lives. This is one of the reasons He gives us stories to share. He desires His name to flow from our lips. Our stories are not about us; they are about Him. Our stories are about Him pursuing our hearts to love Him, worship Him, and serve Him. And, yes, He can even use our sufferings, and often does, to show off His love for us. When your story involves some type of suffering, be sure of this, our stories are not meant to be centered around our

> *Our stories are not about us; they are about Him.*

sufferings, but centered around our God. How He has rescued us from the snare of sin's slavery. How He has been our Provider, our Healer, our Restorer, our Advocate, our Savior, and our Comfort. Our stories should be reflective of the redemptive power of the cross over our lives . . . for eternity.

To my sweet, growing boys,

I cannot tell you how much I desire to surround you with arms of protection at every angle. My mommy heart loves you so deeply that I do not want to see you get hurt or endure pain. Yet I know that the wounds you will incur will be part of the story the Lord is building for your life. And so I am praying now that your spirit will be drawn to prayer and to the Bible when the hurts come your way. I also believe the story God is writing for your life is not meant to be held quietly. As your eyes begin to see the good things the Lord is doing through your seasons of suffering, I pray that your heart will not be able to keep silent. In fact, as you begin to share, I pray you will be amazed at how the Lord will use this courageous step as not only an encouragement to others but also as a comfort to those that hear. Second Corinthians 1:4 states, "He [God] comforts us in all our affliction, so that we may be able to comfort those who are in any kind of affliction, through the comfort we ourselves receive from God." What a beautiful thing the Lord has designed. As He comforts us in our trials and our hurts, He may use our lives as a vessel to display comfort upon others. So, boys, I trust the Lord with your lives. Even though I desire to protect you from pain, I trust that even the stings of this world will be used to glorify Jesus. May the Lord develop within you a strong and courageous spirit to speak boldly of what God is doing in your life. Courageous obedience may not feel monumental, but God is asking for faithful obedience. May your hearts long for more of Jesus . . . always.

I love you!

my heart, mommy

Chapter 11

I Will Not Keep Silent

*"Keeping our eyes on Jesus, the source and perfecter
of our faith, who for the joy that lay before Him
endured a cross and despised the shame
and has sat down at the right hand of God's throne."*
HEBREWS 12:2

New Year's Eve proved to be a pivotal moment in time for me and our friends. We each stepped out in the unknown, making a verbal confession as to how the Lord might be asking us to step out in faith over the coming days, weeks, and months. I knew in my heart that I could no longer shelter all that Jesus had brought me through. I could no longer keep to myself the miracle of experiencing freedom from darkness and the paralyzing "what-if" mind games. I could no longer contain within the walls of my own heart the fact that He breathed life into my physical body multiple times.

I could no longer keep silent His awe-consuming peace
that is greater than the deepest love I know on this earth. I
could no longer keep a tight lip on how Jesus transformed
my affections toward living boldly and intentionally even
in the littlest of moments . . . even in the mundane.

Thank goodness, sharing did not initially take the form
of speaking from a stage. If it had, I might have cowardly
turned in the opposite direction. Rather, my eyes began
to see normal everyday opportunities to be authentic—
whether in more intentional conversations with neighbors,
with families of patients at work, or even within our local
church body. I began letting my guard down and allowing
people into my heart, to witness a glimpse of my daily
battles and how fear no longer enslaves me, sadness no
longer consumes me, and perfectionism and achievement
no longer define me because of my Jesus winning my
affections, my worship, and my life. And, when the Lord
showed up—awakening my eyes and heart and ears to the
eternal—I could no longer hold inside what was meant to
be shared, the powerful saving grace of Jesus Christ.

You might be thinking: *That's great for you, Julie. But
you don't know my suffering. You didn't lose a child. You
didn't lose your husband. You don't have family members
that are in the thick of addiction. You did not struggle with
infertility. You have made it out of the dark pit, but I am
still in the thick of it, and I am not convinced God really
notices my pain. Not only that, but Julie, you do not know
my past.* And you are right. I do not know your past, but
I do know OUR GOD! And I know that our God never
leaves us. The Lord said in Isaiah 43:1–2: "Do not fear, for
I have redeemed you; I have called you by your name; you

are Mine. I will be with you when you pass through the waters, and when you pass through the rivers, they will not overwhelm you. You will not be scorched when you walk through the fire, and the flame will not burn you." Why?! Because the Lord, our God is WITH us.

As women, we spend way too much time comparing. We compare our friendships, our clothes, our children's behaviors, our marriages, our bodies, and even our sufferings. Yes, of course my suffering is different from yours. Hear me out here. Maybe instead of comparing our sufferings, what if we start fighting for one another in the difficult spaces of our lives? Instead of expending energy measuring up to each other's circumstances, why don't we encourage one another by speaking Truth to one another in the midst of our varying sufferings? Instead of focusing on our sufferings, why don't we begin to focus on our God? In the midst of suffering, we will look one of two places. We will either look at the suffering, and we will doubt God; or we will look at God and read the promises of His Word, and it will cause us to cry out to Him in utter desperation, leaning on Him as the One who is able to see us through our circumstances.

It is not my own logical mind-set that convinces me to cling to Jesus. Rather, my desire to control the situation leads me deeper into darkness because I cannot, in fact, control anything at all! Through daily surrendering to Jesus, I find peace. Through the pouring out of His Word over my soul and over my thoughts, I am continually lifted out from the dark pit of sadness and continuous monologues in my head of pondering the "what-if" scenarios. It is through replacing the thoughts of self with thoughts of God my Creator and Jesus—my Savior and hope—that His Light is welcomed over my life. So you may be in a season where you do not want to listen to the Word of God. Or you may be thirsty for Truth to fall on your ears and your heart. Regardless, I am going to speak these Truths, these Promises of God's Word, over you. Why? When I did not want to open my Bible and seek Truth, I had friends in my life that were faithful to share Scripture with me consistently and purposefully. As you read through the following Scriptures, I pray that healing will begin to take place in the areas of your sufferings. I pray that reading the Word of God will bring you glimpses of peace, glimpses of Hope, glimpses of Your Savior who is right in the middle of your circumstance WITH you!

Nothing is too difficult for our God. Genesis 18:14: "Is anything impossible for the LORD?" No. Nothing is impossible for our God. No wound, no void, no form of suffering is too large for our God to heal. In fact, Psalm 147:3 says, "He heals the brokenhearted and binds up their wounds." We can find healing in the arms of Jesus. The Lord God Almighty is able.

*God is **with** us, and He **will** accomplish what He has **promised**. God keeps His Word.* Numbers 23:19: "God is not a man who lies, or a son of man who changes His mind. Does He speak and not act, or promise and not fulfill?" What God says in

His Word, He will accomplish and surely bring it to fruition. God will fulfill what He has promised in His Word. No amendments. No contingency clauses. What God speaks, He will complete.

*We are told to be strong and courageous, for the Lord is **with** us!* Deuteronomy 31:6: "Be strong and courageous; don't be terrified or afraid of them. For it is the LORD your God who goes with you; He will not leave you or forsake you." The Lord is always by our side. He will not leave us. He will not forsake us. We are His daughters, His children; and with Him by our side, we can face even the most dire of circumstances because His presence brings peace which is grander and more powerful than the circumstances of this life on earth. Joshua 1:9: "Haven't I commanded you: be strong and courageous? Do not be afraid or discouraged, for the LORD your God is with you wherever you go."

*His eyes are **on** us, and His ears **hear** our cries!* Psalm 34:15: "The eyes of the LORD are on the righteous, and His ears are open to their cry for help." Our God is the God of compassion. His love for you and for me goes beyond what we could ever wrap our minds around. God Almighty hears our words, our cries, our prayers.

*The Lord is our **help**, our **shield**. May we **trust** His holy name!* Psalm 33:20–21: "We wait for Yahweh; He is our help and shield. For our hearts rejoice in Him because we trust in His holy name." God is Yahweh—He is the I AM; He is Lord. He is our refuge in times of trouble. He is trustworthy because He is God.

*The Lord is our **portion**. In whom shall we place our trust? In whom shall we place our **faith**? We shall place our trust and faith in the **one true, living God**!* Psalm 73:25–26: "Who do I have in heaven but You? And I desire nothing on earth but You. My flesh and my heart may fail, but God is the strength of my heart, my portion forever." God, You are ENOUGH! You are my portion. You are better than all successes, all failures, all sorrows, all victories. Lord, You are sufficient. You meet every need. You alone are simply and fully . . . *enough*!

*The Lord is **compassionate, gracious, loving, and slow to anger**.* Psalm 103:8: "The LORD is compassionate and gracious, slow to anger and rich in faithful love." Yes, Lord, You are rich in mercy. You pour out compassion and grace in faithful love over Your children. Your love is faithful, steady, unchanging, and ever present.

*We cannot escape His **presence**. His **hold** on our hearts and our souls is **unbreakable**.* Psalm 139:7– 12: "Where can I go to escape Your Spirit? Where can I flee from Your presence? If I go up to heaven, You are there; if I make my bed in Sheol, You are there. If I live at the eastern horizon or settle at the western limits, even there Your hand will lead me; Your right hand will hold on to me. If I say, 'Surely the darkness will hide me, and the light around me will be night'—even the darkness is not dark to You. The night shines like the day; darkness and light are alike to You." There is nowhere we can try to run and hide from the Lord. He knows our very being. He knows our every thought. His nearness is for our good.

*We will **not** fear. God is our **refuge and strength!*** Psalm 46:1–3: "God is our refuge and strength, a helper who is always found in times of trouble. Therefore we will not be afraid, though the earth trembles and the mountains topple into the depths of the seas, though its waters roar and foam and the mountains quake with its turmoil." We can trust God to be our Rescuer. We can trust Jesus to bind up our broken hearts. We can trust Jesus to be our strength as we face chemotherapy and medical treatments, financial strains, singleness, marital conflict, defiant children, sudden losses, and even betrayals. His steadfastness overcomes the raging waves of our circumstances. God will not be shaken, and thus we will not be shaken, for He is our Rock upon which we stand and cling. Isaiah 41:10 says, "Do not fear, for I am with you; do not be afraid, for I am your God. I will strengthen you; I will help you; I will hold on to you with My righteous right hand."

*God's Word **revives** us! This is our comfort. His **nearness** is our good.* Psalm 119:50: "This is my comfort in my affliction, Your promise has given me life." Having the Word of the Lord fall upon our ears and penetrate our minds and our hearts will revive our souls to believe and cling to the only thing that is true, right, and just in the midst of the darkness that swarms in this earth.

*Finally, because of Jesus, we can draw **near** to the throne of the Almighty God of grace and mercy.* Hebrews 4:16: "Therefore let us approach the throne of grace with boldness, so that we may receive mercy and find grace to help us at the proper time."

Lord, will You cause our hearts to be softened and responsive to Your Word?. Will the pain we feel in suffering pale in comparison to knowing You, experiencing You, and feeling Your nearness over our lives? As I suffer—as we suffer, Jesus—will You make our hearts know that we are not yet home, and will You cause our hearts to long for home? To be where You created us to live forever—with You in heaven. Amen.

Maybe you are not yet called to write your story down for people to read. Maybe you are not called to stand up on a stage and share your story of suffering with a crowd of people. But I would almost certainly say that each one of you is called to speak the Truth of God's Word to yourself and to the ears and hearts of friends that are desperate for it (and maybe even those who do not yet know that they are desperate for it). Our God is unshakable, and His

Word is unchanging. So, as we find ourselves caught up in a windstorm of chaos, devastation, and desperation, may we cling to the unwavering truth of God's Word to anchor our souls to the One and only immovable God. May we pray His Word, memorize His Word, and speak His Word out loud for our own hearts to hear and for others' hearts to hear.

Boys,

I pray with all my heart that you will each learn to love the Word of God. The Bible is Truth. The Scriptures are God's unfailing Word. I pray that in all seasons of your life you will value the Scriptures and treasure their worth. I pray that you will learn more about Jesus, His redeeming love, His offer of forgiveness and eternal life through faith. May the Holy Spirit fall upon your little lives as God reveals Himself through His Word. May the Bible always be a source of encouragement, hope, conviction, and edification over your lives. I love you more and more each day, but my love pales in comparison to Jesus' love for you.

my heart, mommy

Chapter 12

Jesus Is Better

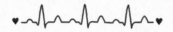

*"Better a day in Your courts than
a thousand anywhere else."*
PSALM 84:10

I absolutely believe it is not only possible for us to experience hope and joy in the midst of suffering but that God desires to show us that He alone is our *only* hope and our *only* source of fulfilling joy. Despite the primary cause leading to our suffering, God promises that He will work every single thing—the hard, the devastating, and the most painful of suffering circumstances—for our good. And, God is a keeper of His promises. My human heart sees all of the suffering, persecution, gut-wrenching violence, and injustices occurring in the world today; and I often wonder, *How in the world will God end up using all of the suffering and evil things in the world for good?* Although I do not know the answer, I do know that God is faithful,

and He is trustworthy. God is a good Father who loves
His children with a jealous love. His love causes our hearts
to trust Him in the midst of grief, fears, and shattered circumstances that make us feel like our world is crumbling
apart. Even when our sufferings occur due to our own sin,
we find forgiveness and hope from the Lord as He restores
our joy through Christ. All the while, if we are honest
with ourselves, He is pruning away the things we worship
more than Him. The Lord desires **all** of our worship—not
fractional worship, not compartmentalized worship, not
convenient worship—yes, He desires *all* of our worship.
And, if anything or anyone is worthy of worship, it is the
God that always was, always is, and always will be. I do
not want to worship something that is temporary. I want
to worship that which is everlasting.

It feels strange for me to say "the older I become"
because at thirty-nine, I really do not feel that old. I
sometimes try to convince myself that I am still in my
twenties. But rest assured, that thought does not stick
around long enough for me to finish typing this sentence.
So the older I become, the more suffering I observe. Not
just monthly or weekly but truly daily. Not only do I
observe suffering in our surrounding community, but
John and I, too often, experience difficult circumstances
in our own lives. But really, who am I to say that we "too
often" experience suffering? Maybe we actually are not
experiencing enough suffering.

Five years ago I stopped asking, "Why? Why does
suffering happen?" The short answer is that we live in
a broken world. Only when we are restored into full
righteousness and the curse of sin is removed as God

intended for His creation, will suffering no longer exist. So we should expect to have our lives interrupted and disrupted by suffering. However, I also do not believe we should even be asking ourselves, "When? When will suffering occur?" Let's be honest, we will drive ourselves into a hole of anxiety, worry, or depression just waiting for something bad to happen or to receive the cancer diagnosis. So, if we stop asking *why* and we stop asking *when*, we ought to be preparing ourselves to answer the question, "In *whom* will we trust as we face suffering?"

How will we respond? Are we going to rest in the Truth of God's Word? Are we going to lean into Jesus and His arms? Are we going to fight the spiritual battles with the armor of God? Are we going to fight with the power of the Holy Spirit? My soul screams out, "YES! ABSOLUTELY! Sign me up! Count me in!" I truly do spend time praying that when the next bout of suffering encroaches into our lives, my soul's response will be victorious over the response of my flesh. Because another battle is raging. That is the battle between our flesh and our soul. One must surrender to the other, and the Holy Spirit within us *does not* surrender to the world. It can't. So I say, "Praise be to God Almighty for His faithfulness." Even when I falter . . . Even in my wandering, the Lord is faithful to grab hold of me and circle my brain back to God's promises rather than dwelling on Julie's version of worldly "wisdom." I long for my every heartbeat and every breath to cry out for His name alone. I want my first response not to be of anger, sadness, frustration, or loneliness. Rather, I desire my instinctual response, the response when no one is looking, to be my heart and my soul crying out the name of my Savior. Yes, I will still feel and express emotions, but I want for my emotions and feelings to be processed through the lens of the gospel.

God has been so gracious to me. He has not once failed to draw near to my life in the midst of suffering. Yes, He has been and continues to be near, even when I do not *feel* Him. And, I have many days and weeks when I do not feel Him. God's character never changes. He is the same yesterday, today, and tomorrow. His Word says He draws near to the brokenhearted (Ps. 34:18), so I believe He, indeed, is near to the brokenhearted. I believe His mercies are new every morning (Lam. 3:22–23) and are given in proportion to one's needs. I believe His nearness is for my good. I believe He will use the suffering for good in my life and to make His name glorified and magnified (Rom. 8:28). I believe that nothing can separate me from His love (Rom. 8:38–39). I believe His peace can guard both my heart and my mind and its thoughts (Phil. 4:7). I believe that no matter the circumstance of this life, I am going to be okay because of Christ, not because of Julie.

> *I believe that no matter the circumstance, I am going to be okay because of Christ.*

As you can imagine, my response typically does not line up with the world's response when I learn of a new cancer diagnosis or another terminal illness. It is not that I do not feel sadness, compassion, or empathy for the one affected

by suffering because I absolutely do. I absolutely feel for
the mommy with young children who is staring cancer in
the face. I absolutely weep alongside a friend whose husband died suddenly on the way home after leaving work
early to take her out on a date. And, I pray exhaustively for
friends that selflessly care for their precious, chronically ill
children as they make yet another trip to the hospital, their
home away from home. Yet, when I wipe the tears away
from my face, I have joy. In the world's eyes, it seems so
strange to have joy. It seems counterintuitive to experience
joy in the midst of such pain and heartache. But this joy is
birthed from believing that I am not home yet. This type of
joy wells up within my heart because I believe that in this
world, "For me, living is Christ and dying is gain" (Phil.
1:21). I have joy knowing that maybe, just maybe, in our
illnesses, in our diseases, in our losses, God might just be
so jealous for us that He wants us to be home.

I know this may sound so extremely insensitive. Please
know that I do not say this flippantly, for I have spent
months processing and grieving through the likelihood of
my own premature death because of my own reality that I
just might not make it to forty, let alone fifty. So for today,
in this very moment, I will simply trust my Savior. Each day
I awaken from sleep, I pray that God will cause my heart
to trust Him once again. To trust Him over my breaths
and my heartbeats. To trust Him to be the caretaker of my
children. And to trust Him to endure my husband until
we all make it into glory with Jesus forever. This trust is
birthed and cultivated through the kindness and gentleness
of the Lord in my life. I believe wholeheartedly that Jesus
desires to show you His trustworthiness, His worth, His

love, and His nearness over your own life so you may be able to proclaim that Jesus is, indeed, better.

The following is a journal entry I wrote in the summer of 2016, as I processed yet another mommy's suffering:

Jen, a warrior and faithful woman—a mother, wife, daughter, and friend. She was and is dearly loved by her family and friends, both near and far. Jen loves Jesus, and she loves her baby boy and her best friend, her husband. Jen is a teacher of God's Word and a mentor to countless women. This is what I know of my friend. A few short weeks ago we gathered to celebrate Jen's life. And, boy was there a celebration—both laughter and tears. Fiery Jen, in the arms of Jesus with no more pain and no more tears and no more suffering. Her faith has become sight. I can nearly hear her squealing with excitement as she laid eyes on her Savior.

Jen was a fighter this side of heaven. A joy-filled fighter. A valiant prayer warrior. If you were to read through her blog entries, documenting her journey through cancer, you would see a beautiful picture of a woman who proclaimed God's faithfulness despite test results and treatment side effects and missing her son's first day of kindergarten.

Jen wrestled between her soul and her heart. She was transparent in this. She wanted to soak up every possible second with the two men in her life—her beloved and their son. I get it. The love of a mother for her babies is one of the most intense, piercing loves I have ever experienced. And whether it is five years or fifty years, it never feels like there is enough time when it comes to "saying good-bye" on this earth. But then I close my eyes and find myself enveloped in brightness and overwhelming peace, and I find myself conflicted. Of course, I would absolutely love to hug and kiss my boys one more time or have the opportunity to share more of myself with them. I do, I do love them so terribly much! But I find myself wanting to leave this party and head to the REAL one. I want to be clear that I do not say this in some place of psychological darkness. I just say this because my soul truly believes that Jesus is better.

Jesus is better than our victories. He is better than our successes and joys this side of heaven.

Jesus is better than the suffering of this world. I know that there are different means for which we encounter suffering on the earth. We live in a fallen world where sin is abundantly rampant. I also know that the enemy is on the prowl to steal, kill, and destroy. No matter the source of our suffering, my eyes see Jesus' pursuit of souls through suffering. Could we dare change our view of suffering? Could we dare find ourselves leaning into Jesus to help us take the blows from suffering rather than build up walls around our hearts to create a fortress of false protection from hurt? Why do we attempt to guard ourselves from vulnerability in the midst of the storm, when Jesus is so delicately pursuing our souls' worship, when we have nothing BUT Him to cling to? Maybe our suffering might just cause us to realize Jesus' true worth? Maybe suffering produces in us a different, more meaningful, more authentic, and soul-penetrating worship? And I don't know about you, but I don't want to show up in heaven and then realize I missed out on knowing and experiencing the depths of my Savior here on this earth. I'm thankful for the hardships of this life. I've actually come to welcome them because I want to watch the power of my Savior in action.

I live every day not knowing if He will give me the next one. Yes, He is sovereign over every single one of my heartbeats. And, when I hear of another mother's death, I often wonder why He breathed life back into me twice. I joke with my friends that if Jesus makes me live into my ninth decade, He will have some explaining to do as to why He made me live for six decades wondering if each day would be my last. I am jealous for heaven. I am jealous to awaken where my faith becomes sight. But, there are days when I sit and wonder if my purpose here and now is to just remind people that we are not home yet. I wonder if my purpose is to share the source of True hope with suffering lives. I wonder if my purpose is to simply live before others with a Jesus-perspective.

Yes, nothing is easy about having to waken without the warmth of your spouse lying beside you in bed. Nothing is easy about missing the sweet, tender voice of your toddler or the high-fives of your teenager. So I sit here today cling-ing to the Truth that Jesus is better, that He will endure me, and that I will see Him face-to-face one day. For those of you who I beat home, I pray you will throw a party, know-ing that I have finally made it to THE party. I want Jesus.

Sweet Boys,

I wrote this journal entry, and I wanted to share it with you because I want you to be confident that Mommy is excited to be with Jesus because He is better. And Jesus wants you to know and believe He is better, too. The Lord is going to allow me to be your mommy here on Earth for the exact number of days

He desires. *I know you will miss me, but know that Jesus loves you more than I ever could with my human heart. And, just as I tell you every night when I tuck you into bed, "I love you to heaven and back," this will never change. I pray nightly for your salvation that we may spend eternity together with God face-to-face. Lord, will You show Yourself to my boys as better than the best of this world. Show them Your worth and endure them through the hard they will face this side of heaven.*

my heart, mommy

Chapter 13

His Purpose

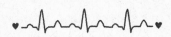

For we are His creation, created in Christ Jesus
for good works, which God prepared ahead
of time so that we should walk in them.
EPHESIANS 2:10

This entire journey has thrown my heart and soul into a wrestling match. As I attempt to process the brevity of my own life coupled with moments of experiencing God's nearness and presence in such tangible ways, I am forced to answer some challenging questions. Do I really believe what I say I believe? Because the question really isn't, "Do I desire to see Jesus more than I desire to walk my boys into school on their first day of kindergarten?" But rather, "Do I long for Jesus so much that I am willing to surrender all of my man-made, Julie-made plans to His All-Knowing-Best Plan for my life?"

For me it comes down to trust. Do I trust Jesus more than I trust myself? Do I believe that God being in control is better than me being in control? Do I believe that following God's leading is better than my own comfort? Do I believe and have faith that He could possibly even use my death for good in my boys' lives? Could He really use the circumstance of losing their mommy to pursue after their souls' affections? Do I believe that God can and will use painful circumstances to show Himself as God, as all-powerful, all-sufficient, and all-loving in my boys' lives? Do I believe and trust that God will not only faithfully comfort my boys and meet their every need but also turn their hearts toward joy, praise, and worship of Him?

The Lord could have simply thrown down the hammer on my self-reliance. Instead, through His love, He showed me that He is reliable. The Lord could have ended my life here on Earth several times. Instead, with much patience, He walks alongside me in love as I face the uncertainty of tomorrow. The Lord could have not allowed my heart muscle to stabilize and, thus, need a heart transplant. But, instead, He chose to stabilize my heart function, and I know that at any point that could change again. There are a lot of things God could have allowed, but He didn't. He obviously still has a purpose for me this side of heaven, and so I do not want to waste any moments in my days. If He brings me home tomorrow,

> *If He brings me home tomorrow, I pray that I am enduring, persevering, and running hard all the way to the finish line of this life.*

I pray that I am enduring, persevering, and running hard all the way to the finish line of this life.

This angst inside me to live purposefully and intentionally plays out in the decisions John and I make as a married couple and as a family. We do our best to make choices that communicate to our children and our friends that we are fully present with them, not distracted by technology or our own agendas. We do not do this perfectly. In fact, we have a lot of room for growth. A lot of room for growth! In the times I catch myself completing tasks *I* feel *need* to be done that actually *do not need* to be completed in that moment, I am often convicted to get back on the floor and play with my kids. After all, the laundry can wait.

Every day when I awaken and I begin to feel my heart beat in an abnormal rhythm, I could tend to hoard all of my moments for myself. Yet the Lord did not allow me to develop heart failure and a life-threatening heart rhythm so that I would turn inward and remain solely self-focused. No, God has not called me to the sidelines. He has simply given me a heart that depends on Him to make it beat every heartbeat and squeeze enough blood out each contraction to meet my body's needs—the same as yours. And He still calls me to walk in faith and service toward others. Our sufferings do not negate God's call on our life to love Him and love others. And, as we love the Lord and love on others, God shows up and reveals more of Himself to our hearts.

> *Our sufferings do not negate God's call on our life to love Him and love others.*

Probably each one of us knows exactly where we were and what we were doing the morning of September 11, 2001. If asked, not as many of us could recall the details of our environment and the smells of where we were when we learned of the devastating earthquake that crumbled the country of Haiti on January 12, 2010. However, for me? I remember. I was standing in my kitchen cleaning another round of bottles at the kitchen sink with thoughts of what to fix my little ones for dinner when I turned on the television for the first time that day. Honestly, I was more interested in having some background noise in the house than catching up on the day's news. But then the headline scrolling at the bottom of the screen caught my eye. I discovered that earlier in the afternoon, a catastrophic, 7.0 magnitude earthquake struck Port-au-Prince, Haiti. It was only a matter of hours before major media outlets were on the ground reporting raw, heart-aching images of the devastation Haiti was enduring.

Suddenly a country everyone had forgotten was televised and broadcast across all media outlets around the globe. I immediately responded, "I need to go. I have to help. I need to be there to help take care of the injured, the dying." This is simply how I am wired. I am wired to respond in the midst of the emergencies and the life-and-death scenarios. And it did not matter to me that my heart was failing or that my heart muscle was functioning at only half of what would be considered normal. All I knew was that I needed to go. The people of Haiti were in desperate need, and they did not have enough hands to care for all of the injured people. I simply needed to go. For me it was black-and-white.

Enter John. John all but duct-taped me to a chair to keep me from hopping on the next flight to Haiti. After all, I was less than three months removed from having my ICD placed in my chest, and my heart function was still poor. Knowing this, John's voice of reason directed my efforts (and heightened passions) stateside to aid some close friends of ours that were teaming with a local church in town to provide relief. Our friends spearheaded the effort organizing medical teams and donated medical supplies to be sent down to an established mission organization on the ground in Haiti. This mission organization urgently, as did all organizations in the area, set up a tent hospital on its property adjacent to its already established clinic and pharmacy. Needless to say, my emotional fight-or-flight response to the devastation slowly transitioned into a more logical response. Over the course of the following several weeks, I spent days helping to inventory medical supplies that were donated by various hospitals throughout Austin, and joined the effort of packing the supplies to be transported by weekly medical teams that were formed within a moment's notice.

John witnessed my heart's burden continue to burn for the opportunity to make the trip and use my hands in Haiti. His protective hand and love released me from solely helping in the relief efforts stateside. With his blessing, I placed my name on one of the upcoming medical teams that would go into the trenches of Haiti. I was overjoyed and scared at the same time because I knew I would be risking my own health. But I had to help. I just had to go help.

And I did.

The Lord could have allowed me to serve the people of Haiti unseen from a windowless room in the basement of the church building in Austin, Texas, sorting medical supplies—which, in itself, was great. Sometimes we are called to be behind the scenes where our prayers reach the throne of God and powerful things happen by the hand of God. However, this time the Lord also brought me to Haiti to serve on the front lines. I would be remiss if I did not mention that I went with my own plan of wanting to serve the sick, the injured, and the broken. But God—but God, right?!—took my small, narrow-focused agenda and actually used my time in Haiti for the continued healing of my own brokenness. Isn't that just God's nature to do a work in our own hearts as we serve? Despite being used as the hands and feet of Jesus to those in the tent hospital and community clinic, I am in awe that Jesus might just have accomplished more work in my own soul than my hands did in serving. My hope is that despite whatever circumstance you find yourself in, you would know that your life has a purpose . . . to be used by God simply by being willing to say yes to whatever He is asking of you. Trusting, stepping out in faith, believing that God is enough, and clinging to what you know is true about God's character. Say yes to Him and watch Him move.

Boys,

God has created each one of us for and with a purpose, a calling. Scripture clearly states that God formed our hearts, souls, minds, and bodies that we might worship Him with our lives. He has purposed our lives—your life, my life—so that we would share the life of Jesus with others. Our sufferings neither lessen nor make null the purpose given to us by the living God. Our sufferings do not afford us the opportunity to leave the armor of God hanging in the closet. No! Despite the circumstances of this life, we daily need the belt of Truth, the breastplate of righteousness, the gospel of peace, the shield of faith, the helmet of salvation, and the sword of the Spirit. Because God might just use our sufferings to produce a greater form of worship and more focused intentionality in living out each day for His name. Lord, I pray You will give my boys the vision to see Your purpose for their lives. May You persevere them in every circumstance they face.

my heart, mommy

Chapter 14

Haiti

"LORD, You have searched me and known me.
You know when I sit down and when I stand up;
You understand my thoughts from far away.
You observe my travels and my rest;
You are aware of all my ways.
Before a word is on my tongue,
You know all about it, LORD.
You have encircled me;
You have placed Your hand on me.
This extraordinary knowledge is beyond me.
It is lofty; I am unable to reach it."
PSALM 139:1–6

With John's blessing I sought to join one of the next available medical teams traveling to Port-au-Prince, Haiti. The team in need of more nurses would depart in just a few weeks. The only kicker was that this particular team was comprised of medical professionals primarily from Indiana, with the exception of one other nurse (besides me) traveling from Austin. Despite the initial uneasiness of not knowing a single soul going on the trip and the challenging logistics of somehow connecting with complete strangers upon arriving in a developing foreign country, John and I were so grateful to learn that the team would include a seasoned cardiologist from Indiana—a grace of our sovereign God.

John and I awoke hours before dawn so I could catch a flight that departed at the same time the sun would peak its head over the horizon. As John and I drove to the airport, we found ourselves in that space of comfortable silence . . . and not simply because we were still half asleep. We listened to several songs from the *Passion: Awakening* CD. We gripped each other's hand so tightly as we worshipped together.

With the moon still hanging high in the sky, we pulled up to the departure lanes at the airport terminal. Ours was a tearful good-bye. Not in the sense that John was sending me off to war, but rather cased in an understanding of the risk involved, mostly surrounding my health. Any illness I might acquire had the potential to cause increased damage to my heart muscle. Yet, when the Holy Spirit provides conviction to move, we must obey. After an embrace where neither one of us wanted to be the first to loosen our grip, I took a few deep breaths and entered the airport with my hiking backpack secured over both shoulders. The airport was quite sparse. I intentionally made a beeline to the women's restroom so I could collect myself and dry my eyes before having any other human interaction, say, with the TSA security personnel. However, I am not sure I successfully covered up my emotional good-bye to my beloved, given that the whites of my eyes were rather pink and swollen.

As I made my way through security, I gathered up my belongings, relaced my running shoes, and began to wander down the hallways of the Austin airport. My ten-day adventure had officially begun before I even set foot on the first of my three flights that day. The emotions of saying good-bye to John slowly faded and were replaced with nervous excitement. Reality began to set in that I actually took a step of faith not knowing where my foot was going to land.

Some would say this journey was courageous; however, I did not feel the least bit brave. Others might have called me foolish, and I might agree with them if I had solely measured the risks without taking into consideration the trustworthiness of our God. Yes, I felt nervous. I was not sure what I was about to face. I could not predict what my body and heart were going to experience. Heck, I did not even know the names and faces of the other people on my team. What in the world was I doing?! What in the world was I thinking?! Yet, in

> Some would say this journey was courageous; however, I did not feel the least bit brave.

that moment, what I knew of God was that He is strength and He is all-knowing. He would be enough. Surely, God would be enough. "Lord," I begged, "You *have* to be enough! No, really Lord, You *have to be enough!*"

God, in His pure goodness, had a fun surprise waiting for me at the departing gate. My darling, sweet friend, Kim! Kim is the friend that talked me down off the ledge when I was nervous to go out on a first date with John. Yes, she is *that* friend. The friend that is not scared to call me out when she sees me believing lies from the enemy and not believing in the Truth of God's Word. We all need a Kim in our lives. Kim and I were "randomly" booked on the same flight to Dallas. The Lord certainly did not have to orchestrate placing such a sweet and dear friend on the same flight that morning, but in His kindness He did.

> "You **have** to be enough! No, really Lord, You **have to be enough!**"

Now the great thing about traveling on a 6:00 a.m. flight out of Austin was that the flight was not overbooked. Kim and I were able to relocate from our assigned seating and find a row where we could sit together. In true Kim form she talked my ear off the entire flight. As she has done time and time again over the life of our friendship, she shared the Truth of Scripture with me and prayed over me. Just before we parted ways to find our connecting gates in Dallas, I told her that Jesus spoke peace over me through our not so coincidental time together at thirty thousand feet. Yes, Lord, Kim and I could not have planned a better early morning coffee date, even if we tried.

Off to Miami I went, where I hoped somehow to connect with all the other members of our medical team. The
Miami airport was as crowded as the New York subway
system during the evening commute. There were literally
hundreds of people crowding around the departing gate to
Haiti. Every seat in the boarding area was occupied with
what seemed like just as many people sitting on the floor
clumped together near all the available outlets, giving their
cell phones one last opportunity to be charged. Needless
to say, the swarming crowd made it more than challenging
to identify which group of folks appeared as if they might
be headed to Mission of Hope. And, it certainly did not
appear that a group T-shirt was made saying, "Hey Julie
Manning, You're with US!" Every last one of the five-
hundred-plus passengers were headed down to volunteer
in relief and medical work, so I gave up on the idea of asking each individual exactly where they were headed when
arriving in Haiti. But there was one woman. One woman
who was pacing back and forth on the outskirts of the
crowd. One woman who appeared to be traveling alone.
So I approached her, introduced myself, and asked if this
was her first trip to Haiti. When she mentioned that she
was from Austin, Texas, I asked with a voice of hopeful
desperation, "I know that this is a random question, but
are you by any chance headed to Mission of Hope to work
with a medical team from Indiana?" Her eyes expressed
just as much relief as my heart experienced when she nearly
shouted, "Yes!! Yes, I am!" Joan and I became fast friends
in the thirty seconds we conversed before being asked to

board the aircraft. We sat at opposite ends of the plane. But at least we each had a familiar face to look for once we arrived. Joan and I would have plenty of time over the next week to get to know one another as we served side by side.

I used the relatively short flight to Port-au-Prince to pull out my journal and pray. As I began to write, my heart just simply exploded on paper:

April 10, 2010

Oh, Jesus, You are so kind. I just looked up and noticed the man sitting directly in front of me studying a book about orthopedic injuries. Of the hundreds of physicians and medical professionals on the flight, you placed this specific man, Dr. Terry, right in front of me. Not only is he a family practice physician who has traveled to Haiti monthly since the earthquake, but Dr. Terry is the physician leading the Indiana group to Mission of Hope! Thank you, Lord, for providing this brief conversation with Terry to set up a guardian for me once we arrive in Haiti!

Fill my heart with increasing joy as this travel day continues. Within my spirit, bring energy, perseverance, resiliency, humility, and a positive attitude. I ask for Your angels to surround me and to go out before me. I ask for Your protection over my health. I pray for rest when the opportunity arises.

Lord, will You change me for good? Use my hands as only You can. Help me touch and impact the lives of those I care for, those I meet, those I merely pass by. Make my heart available to experience what You have in store for me, not only physically and emotionally, but spiritually. May Your Word always be on my heart and mind. From You, Lord,

I will gain strength. And, when I tire, help me remember that those here on the ground are also tired and have not rested since the day of the earthquake. Keep my mind from thinking about myself. Keep my mind focused on the goal set before me: to love these people, sacrificing myself for their good.

As I read back over what I prayed that day, I get goose bumps over my body when I contemplate the reality of how the Lord not only answered those prayers, but He prompted my spirit to ask for the very specific things that I would need over the coming hours and days.

My eyes saw too much in Haiti. Really, it was too much. The pain went deep, too deep. My heart could not help but embrace the pain and utter heartbreak of the patients I cared for in the tent-like hospital. One sweet woman was bedridden with a crushed ankle and a crushed right wrist and forearm. She was holding her newborn baby girl in her right arm when her home collapsed due to the earthquake's brutal destruction. Not only did her newborn die in her embrace, but she also lost her husband who sacrificed his body to shield their toddler's vibrant life from the caving roof and walls. And yet, as Thelisma shared her story with me through the use of an interpreter, she slowly and gently placed her left hand on the Bible, which never moved from within reach. Her expression hinted at a smile. Her soul found joy despite the saddening loss of those she loved most because of what she had found in Jesus.

My eyes saw souls turn toward repentance. My eyes witnessed grace-filled forgiveness. I was unable to leave the bedside of one man who just days before my arrival underwent surgery on one of his lower legs. He had earned the nickname "Broken Man" because he had more than fifteen broken bones in his upper and lower extremities. Sadly, infection had made a home in his leg that had spread into his blood system. Broken Man was now fighting for life and nearing his last breaths. Had he been stateside, he would have no doubt been in intensive care. But in Haiti, he was lying four feet from a young mother holding her toddler daughter with far less severe injuries. I did all I knew how to do, medically speaking, to keep him alive until the morning. And, as the realization of how extremely sick he was sank in, Broken Man confessed to me his unfaithfulness to his wife who had never once left his side despite the multiple affairs. He was in so much pain that he drifted in and out of slumber for only minutes at a time throughout the entire night. At one point he motioned for me to come nearer to hear his whisper. In between taking his blood pressure every five minutes and administering additional IV antibiotics and IV fluids, I heard him whisper, "Please tell my wife how sorry I am. If I die before she awakens in the morning, please tell my wife I love her."

My eyes saw miraculous, unexplainable healing. There was a teenage girl who had been a patient since nearly the first day that the tent hospital was constructed. She was in queue to have an amputation performed of her lower leg because of a crush injury to her ankle. In fact, she was at the top of the list for our surgical team. One of the nurses from Indiana asked this young girl if several of us could pray for her before she was taken back into the operating area. So three of us encircled the end of her bed, gently laying hands on her leg, and asked God to move in her life, to give her the strength and courage to persevere through the surgery and recovery. We asked that God would work a miracle in her life. Just as we said, "Amen," the surgeon walked up to take one more assessment of her ankle. Something prompted him to take one additional X-ray of the girl's leg, even though he held in his hand the X-ray film taken just three days prior. All I can say is that this young lady did not undergo an amputation that afternoon. Instead, one of the physical therapists had her out of bed, practicing how to walk on a leg that had not held her weight in walking since the day of the earthquake. As for her X-ray, you might ask? Well, it showed completely healthy and well-formed anklebones. We had asked for God to work a miracle in her life and, although we were praying for her salvation, God certainly worked a miracle in healing this sweet teenage girl's ankle.

Each of our circumstances has the ability to change us as people, impacting our lives as we walk around on this earth. We can live viewing our circumstances through the lens of Jesus and the good news, or we can live with a self-focused mind-set. Without God's redemptive love over my life, I would no doubt live with the latter view. But the reality is that Jesus has saved me, and now I cannot help but view this world with Him being the center of it all

. . . not just in the victories and the successes but even in
the messiness. Even in the devastating losses. Even in the
crushing of hearts.

My intention upon going to Haiti was to serve and
share Jesus in the messiness without expecting anything
in return. I wanted to help. I wanted to be available to do
whatever needed to be done. I wanted to take care of the
hurting. I wanted to pray for people. I wanted to be used
by God. But then I met a young teenager. At the time
Jean Marc was fourteen years old. I soon realized that
God had a special, tender gift for my soul through this
growing boy. Each day after school Jean Marc came to the
tent hospital to serve as an interpreter for us. Each day he
would enter the "Dome," as we referred to the inpatient
ward, with laughter and loud, joyful singing. His voice was
a refreshing and welcome sound to our ears. Jean Marc's
English was pristine, yet we nurses had a tad bit of fun
teaching him some slang terms along the way.

Because I do not do surface conversation well, it took
me all of three minutes before asking Jean Marc to tell me
his story. I wanted to know more about this kid and how
he came to live in the orphanage at Mission of Hope. Jean
Marc shared that he grew up without a father. His mother
worked hard to provide food and schooling for him. After
becoming ill in his early childhood, Jean Marc's mother
passed away. Shortly after her death he was accepted into
the orphanage at Mission of Hope where he learned about
Jesus. Since then Jesus had taken hold of Jean Marc's soul
and set him on fire to share the gospel with joy and without
a hint of hesitation in any and every conversation.

One afternoon I was going from bed to bed changing bandages and cleaning out wounds. As I made my way toward the back of the Dome to gather the supplies I needed for the next patient, I heard Jean Marc entering through the back of the tent. With his backpack loosely thrown over one shoulder, he was dancing and singing— rather, shouting—a praise song with his arms waving back and forth in the air. His voice echoed throughout the ward that was the size of a football field. Soon many of the patients began smiling as they heard the singing of this youthful boy with his awkwardly changing voice. With a smile on my face, my eyes glistened as I just stopped to observe this teen boy worshipping His God. And then it hit me. Out of nowhere this inner voice began, "Hey Julie. Guess what! You do not have to be alive for ME to grab hold of your boys' hearts. I, the Lord Jesus, will win their worship regardless of your being present to raise them. And you know what else? I will use the timing of your death for good in their lives, and it will be a part of their story on how I am pursuing after them. Because, I LOVE THEM MORE. My plan for them is better than anything you could attempt to orchestrate."

Oh, yes. I slowly lowered my body down to the ground, leaning up against the metal shelving units housing gauze and bandages. And. I. Wept.

Really, Lord? You just had to take me to Haiti, didn't You? Yes, You needed to take me to Haiti. Yes, I came to serve. Yes, I came to pour out my heart on this group of people. Yes, I came to work sixteen plus hours a day. Yes, I came to pray and share the gospel of Jesus. Yet God showed Himself to me through Jean Marc, an awkwardly dancing and singing fourteen-year-old boy. Yes, God used Jean Marc to calm my biggest fear of leaving my boys without their mommy.

My hope is that we all will live in such a way that our lives reflect the light of Christ and the joy of knowing Him as we live and express the often hard emotions that accompany suffering. *Lord, please help me not to waste today. Help me live purposefully, presently, and intentionally so others who are in the darkness of suffering will be reminded to taste Your joy, Your light, Your nearness, and Your pursuit of their soul. So that our eyes might witness You bringing beauty from ashes.*

> *My hope is that we reflect the light of Christ and the joy of knowing Him as we live and express the hard emotions that accompany suffering.*

Boys,

You know I love you. These words flow from my lips as often as they are present in my thoughts. If the Lord wills and He allows me to watch you grow from little boys to young men, then I will continue to speak these words over you. You may grow tired of hearing me say, "I love you to heaven and back." You might even become embarrassed in middle school if I share these words with you in front of your friends. But you must know, I will never stop saying them to you because these words are true.

You also know that my love is imperfect. I often find myself asking you for forgiveness because I do not always love you well. There are times I raise my voice or discipline out of anger rather than love. And though my love is bound by the boundaries of imperfection, God's love for you is perfect. His love for you far exceeds the capacity of my human heart. He formed you. He breathed life into your bodies and your souls. His love never fails, and His love never gives up. His love endures all things. His perfect love has formed the best plan for your life as He works out your sanctification. And so I must, in return, trust that His love over your life is deeper and better than my love ever will be . . . because His love is without flaw. May your life forever rest in His arms of love.

my heart, mommy

Chapter 15

Beauty from Ashes

"The Spirit of the Lord GOD is on Me, because the LORD has anointed Me to bring good news to the poor. He has sent Me to heal the brokenhearted, to proclaim liberty to the captives and freedom to the prisoners; to proclaim the year of the Lord's favor, and the day of our God's vengeance; to comfort all who mourn, to provide for those who mourn in Zion; to give them a crown of beauty instead of ashes, festive oil instead of mourning, and splendid clothes instead of despair. And they will be called righteous trees, planted by the LORD to glorify Him."
ISAIAH 61:1–3

When our team arrived in Port-au-Prince, we traveled by school bus to the small village where Mission of Hope is located. Since we landed late afternoon, the bright sun allowed our eyes to take in all of the environmental surroundings over our ninety-minute drive. There were moments of complete silence on the bus. Moments when every last one of us sank into our seats and stared at the devastation. The bus weaved around collapsed buildings that were partially blocking roads. Much of the rubble unmoved, untouched since the day of the earthquake. We drove past areas where hundreds of small, royal blue tarps, propped up with sticks and cinderblocks, were converted into shelter for displaced families. Those ninety minutes sobered every one of our hearts. Television reporters can display images on the nightly news, but seeing the things we saw with our own eyes brought an entirely new depth to the realities the Haitians were facing. It can be challenging to truly grasp the suffering of others unless you are living through it with them. Or living it yourself.

The sun was setting as the bus turned down the dirt road leading up to the gate at Mission of Hope. Upon arriving, Joan and I learned that we would work the night shift in the tent hospital *that very night*. Our shift would begin as soon as we could change into our scrubs. Who needs sleep, right? Together, we persevered through an exhaustive night. However, what our eyes saw around 5:00 a.m. was worth every last bit of fatigue. As the sky began to reveal the beauty of the impending sunrise, we noticed the beautiful dirt hills and landscape on the horizon. There was beauty. There was calming peace. The hills had not just suddenly appeared. The hills and the landscape were present the previous day for our eyes to see from the school bus windows. Yet our eyes truly only saw the hurt and the pain. It wasn't until Joan and I had endured through the darkness of the night that our eyes could see the beauty of the morning. The beauty of what was in the background. Perspective. Haiti offered me that perspective. A turning point for my heart.

Suffering has the ability to do something incredibly beautiful within our hearts and souls, doesn't it? When Jesus gives us perspective, our eyes can begin to see through the pain and suffering and view the landscape of how He is weaving in beauty in spite of the pain.

One morning, in the quietness of children soundly sleeping, I poured my morning coffee into one of my favorite coffee mugs and grabbed my Bible from the kitchen counter. I took a seat near the windows that look out into our backyard, and I opened up the Word, turning to the Psalms. I was not particularly down emotionally that morning, but I knew my soul needed to read something in the Scriptures that would encourage me; otherwise my thoughts might have spiraled down into a darker place. I needed God's Word to be at the forefront of my mind so I could battle the deceiving thoughts I knew might crouch at the door. The pages of my Bible naturally opened to Psalm 42. Not because I intentionally sought out to read Psalm 42, but rather because I had randomly shoved a note that I was given weeks prior into the middle of my Bible after church one Sunday. It was no coincidence that my soul really needed to read and meditate on Psalm 42 on this early summer morning:

> [1]As a deer longs for streams of water,
> so I long for You, God.
> [2]I thirst for God, the living God.
> When can I come and appear before God?
> [3]My tears have been my food day and night,
> while all day long people say to me,
> "Where is your God?"

⁴I remember this as I pour out my heart:
how I walked with many,
leading the festive procession to the house of God,
with joyful and thankful shouts.

⁵Why am I so depressed?
Why this turmoil within me?
Put your hope in God, for I will still praise Him,
my Savior and my God.
⁶I am deeply depressed;
therefore I remember You from the land of Jordan
and the peaks of Hermon, from Mount Mizar.
⁷Deep calls to deep in the roar of Your waterfalls;
all Your breakers and Your billows have swept
    over me.
⁸The Lord will send His faithful love by day;
His song will be with me in the night—
a prayer to the God of my life.

⁹I will say to God, my rock,
"Why have You forgotten me?
Why must I go about in sorrow
because of the enemy's oppression?"
¹⁰My adversaries taunt me,
as if crushing my bones,
while all day long they say to me,
"Where is your God?"
¹¹Why am I so depressed?
Why this turmoil within me?
Put your hope in God, for I will still praise Him,
my Savior and my God.

The NASB version of verse 11 says, "Why are you in despair, O my soul? And why have you become disturbed within me? Hope in God, for I shall yet praise him, the help of my countenance and my God."

There are times when I read through the book of Psalms and I cannot fully relate to David's prayers regarding enemies. Maybe I am naïve, but I do not feel like I have enemies in the world that are seeking my life. However, I am confident in stating that I do have a spiritual enemy that is seeking to destroy my soul's love of my Savior, Jesus. Psalm 42 reminded me that circumstances of this life have occurred and will continue to occur that will discourage my soul. This is reality for all of us. There will be moments when our children do not listen or do not want to participate in family prayer time. Shoot, our kids might just be downright defiant. There will be times when someone we trust does something that disappoints us or even betrays us. There will be times when the doctor gives a poor prognosis rather than a hope for a cure. All of these things can lean our hearts and minds toward discouragement and even despair. So where is our encouragement in this? Psalm 42 states a command to our souls. "I will put my hope in God! I will praise Him again!" It is as if the author admits, "Hey! Stop being discouraged! Stop being downtrodden. HOPE in the One who authors HOPE! Hope in the One who SAVES! Hope in the One who is not our enemy but the pursuer of our soul's worship and love and affection. Hope in the One who desires an everlasting relationship with us. Hope in the ONE that does not disappoint. Hope in the ONE who created us for Himself."

We have a choice. We have a decision to make. Remain or hope. Remain in discouragement. Remain in our sorrows. Remain in the sting of the pain. Remain in a state of belief that the lies the enemy feeds us are somehow true. OR hope in our Savior. Yes, I am imploring each one of us not merely to spend time contemplating hope or dialoging about what it might look like to actually hope. Rather, just do it. Just HOPE in Jesus. Hope in His saving grace. Hope in the blood of the Lamb. Hope in the One who has a place for us where the enemy may no longer dwell around us. Hope in the One whose Spirit can cover your body in goose bumps when the Holy Spirit shows up in your life. Hope in the One who does not need our perfect performance but whose performance on the cross was the perfect, finishing work.

Hope in the One who does not need our perfect performance but whose performance on the cross was the perfect, finishing work.

Hope in the Word of God that is sharper than a double-edged sword and does not go out and return void. Make the mental decision to hope until your emotions can catch up with your mind.

I have too many times remained in the valley and remained in the darkness wallowing in the pain. The darkness of my circumstances swallowed any possible flicker of light. Slowly over time I became more comfortable staying in the darkness instead of raising my eyes toward the light. It seemed easier to keep my head buried in my hands than muster the courage to want to find joy again. But then the whisper entered my ears even though my eyes were shut tight, "Julie, your circumstances do not rule over your God. The Light of the Lord does not come and go. He is always Light. He is never dark. Julie, lift your eyes to see His Light. You may not feel the warmth of His light over you right now, but rest assured that He is near."

I cannot help but want to shout out loud, "PREACH!" when I read through 2 Corinthians 4. Paul is writing to the Corinthians in verses 6–18:

> For God who said, "Let light shine out of darkness," has shone in our hearts to give the light of the knowledge of God's glory in the face of Jesus Christ. Now we have this treasure in clay jars, so that this extraordinary power may be from God and not from us. We are pressured in every way but not crushed; we are perplexed but not in despair; we are persecuted but not abandoned; we are struck down but not destroyed. . . . Therefore we do not give up. Even though our outer person is being destroyed, our inner person is being renewed day by day. For our momentary light affliction is producing for us an absolutely incomparable eternal weight of glory. So we do not focus on what is seen, but on what is unseen. For what is seen is temporary, but what is unseen is eternal.

I want to cry out, "Julie, don't you get it?!" I want to ask others, "Don't you get it?!" Yes, I know this will cause some offense. I know this will fall on ears not wanting to hear. I know you may just stop reading right here and not continue. I know you may be thinking, *Julie, I am just hurting TOO much! Do not minimize my hurt. Do not minimize my circumstances.* Remember, I am saying this to myself, too. Like you I am a flawed person who continues to wrestle. And I need you to know that my intent is not to minimize your wounds, your hurts, your sufferings, or your circumstances. Rather, I desire to proclaim the BIGness, the GREATness, the HUGEness, the TRUSTworthiness, and the insurmountable VALUE and WORTHiness of our GOD! To you and to me.

When we shift our focus to living for and hoping in the unseen, our focus will naturally dim on that which is seen and the suffering in this life.

When we shift our focus to living for and hoping in the unseen, our focus will naturally dim on that which is seen and the suffering in this life. For what is seen is temporary. Our suffering is temporary. Our suffering is passing. Our suffering has nothing on our God who has always been and will always be.

Hope in Christ. Hope as if you actually will obtain that for which you hope. Speak to your soul. "Soul, why are you discouraged?! Stop believing that your suffering will bring defeat, and start hoping in Christ that He will actually bring good from the darkness and beauty from the ashes. Trust and hope in Jesus to bring upon healing, provision, restoration, forgiveness, and fulfilling joy. Praise His name!" And tell your discouragement to get on with its fleeting self. This life and its circumstances are just that—fleeting.

Boys,

There will be times in your lives when you will just have to pull up your bootstraps and decide in your mind to kick the lies the enemy feeds you to the curb and speak the Truth of God's Word over your circumstances. Instead of wallowing in your disappointments or failures or self-pity, you will actually need to make a conscious decision and move away from your emotions. Sometimes you will be your own barrier to experiencing the joy and hope of Christ. When you find yourself in that place . . . when you become your own roadblock . . . YOU need to move! You need to spend more time reading God's Word rather than meditating on the same depressive thoughts that run through your mind. Replace your man-centered thoughts with God-centered Truth. Beg the Lord for more and more faith to believe in the Scriptures. Take a step toward Jesus and a step away from your flesh. Choose to hope in that which we know is true and not the words of the world that are tossed in the wind. Edward Mote wrote the hymn "My Hope Is Built" back in the 1800s. I pray these words will speak to your soul, "My hope is built on nothing less than Jesus' blood and righteousness. I dare not trust the sweetest frame, but wholly lean on Jesus' name."[3] Boys, I pray you will run to the King of kings. I pray you will worship the Lord Almighty with every ounce of your being. I pray you will have the courage to pray in the power of the Holy Spirit. I pray against complacency in your life. I pray that your heart and your mind will place hope in the God who fulfills His promises. Lord, will You reveal Your Hope, Your complete Joy, Your Worthiness, Your Love to my boys—Your sons.

my heart, mommy

Chapter 16

Why Go There?

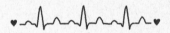

"Then Moses said to the people, 'Remember this day when you came out of Egypt, out of the place of slavery, for the LORD brought you out of here by the strength of His hand.'"
EXODUS 13:3

So, why even share all of this? Why was my spirit making my belly twist into knots until I exhaled the words, "I think I am supposed to share my story"? Because this book, this story, is not about some girl with a heart problem. It's not a book about some blue-eyed, blonde, curly-haired girl's circumstances. My prayer is that each one of these pages does one thing only: encourage you to lift your head long enough to see the bigness of God, the brightness of His Light, the abundance of our Heavenly Father's amazing love, the relentless and purposeful pursuit of *your* soul by Jesus, and the power of the Holy Spirit within your life.

We share our stories to remember God's faithfulness. We share our stories to direct our hearts back to what is important in this life as we feel the tug to drift away from a surrendered posture unto the Lord to a life of self-sufficiency. This life is not about us. Rather, this life is about Jesus. This life is not about our individual lives but about the day when the entire big "C" Church body is in the same place at the same time for eternity surrounding the throne of God, proclaiming "Holy, holy, holy, Lord God, the Almighty" (Rev. 4:8). We are not yet home, but rest assured, we WILL be home one day. Until then we must battle against complacency and against comfort and against taking things into our own hands of control. Even when we seek Jesus fervently. Even when we rely on the Lord for every ounce of energy and sustaining breath. Even when we spend countless hours begging for healing and increasing faith, our sinful nature will have a magnetic pull to turn our focus back onto ourselves. Maybe I am just describing myself here, but I do not think that is the case. As the hardest, most intense season of suffering becomes ever so slightly further and further from the present day, our lives slowly shift one degree at a time back toward self-sustainment and away from complete and utter dependence upon Jesus—who, by the way, authored our faith in the first place. And so we share our stories so that

> *We share our stories to remember all the Lord has done and to keep our hearts anchored to the cross.*

we remember because we *need* to remember. We *must* remember.

As we feel ourselves drifting, we may still confess our need for Christ. Sure, we may still pray and open the Bible some, if not most, days. Our soul may cry out, "Amen!" to the worship songs we sing on Sunday mornings or as we drive our kids to school, affirming our belief in the words sung over the *family-friendly* radio station.

But life is different, right? As I sit here several years after the most intense season of suffering, my day does not look exactly the same as it did the day I awakened to view burn marks on my chest or the morning when I collapsed in front of dozens of toddlers in the nursery. It is not that my need for Jesus has changed—not one bit. My need for Jesus was exactly the same then as it is now and will be tomorrow. However, my keen awareness of my need has been dimmed. And, frankly, that scares me. I do not want to live with a faded, less intense realization of my daily need for Christ.

How do we keep the desperation for Jesus? How do we maintain the focus on the here and now between seasons of suffering? After all, suffering is not a one-time occurrence. Amen?! The longer we live, the more suffering we will experience within our own lives. We will also observe affliction in the lives of those around us and in the lives of people all over the world. As I look back over ten years of our marriage, John and I have suffered through a miscarriage, being a victim of financial fraud, the loss of our seventeen-month-old nephew, and most recently the flooding of our home, leaving us displaced for eight months as we rebuilt the home from the ground up. And then there has been the last six-plus years of living with chronic heart disease and the constant reminder of it all as I feel the flip-flopping of my heart inside my chest and feel the edges of my defibrillator underneath the skin of my chest wall. Yet I know this is not the end of the suffering. More will come.

In lieu of all of this, how do we live intentionally today with the purpose of living for Jesus? We remember. We remember what Jesus has done. We remember what Jesus IS doing. We remember what Jesus said He WILL do, which is come back to get us! Yes, we remember. We ask Jesus for more faith. We ask the Holy Spirit to move in power. We read the Bible, the very breath of God Almighty, and we are reminded of all that He has done since creation. After all, our generation is not the only generation that must be persistent in remembering. For every generation before us and for every generation to come, we must remember.

Remember the Israelites in the Old Testament? They were God's chosen people. For goodness' sake, how many times did the Israelites turn to worship idols just moments after God demonstrated His power? How many times did they question God after He displayed His provision? How many times did they doubt God's nearness just moments after the Lord, time and time again, showed His faithfulness? And how many times did the Israelites turn away from the Lord when the Lord did not give them what they wanted? We are prideful to think we would not have strayed, doubted, or questioned God had we been the ones who walked across dry land as God parted the Red Sea. I know my heart; I would have wandered. Heck, I do wander and am going to guess that you wander, too. Remember the disciples in the New Testament? We might think that if only we could have touched the hands and side of the resurrected Jesus, like Thomas did, we would not stray. Realistically, we would have the same struggle. The Israelites wandered. The disciples wandered. I wander. Each one of us needs to be consistently and continually reminded of God's redemption story.

We can only view this life through the lens of the gospel of Jesus to the extent in which we know and believe the gospel itself. If we are not spending time reading the Bible, studying the Scriptures, and meditating on the Truth of God's Word, then how can we even begin to walk through life living out the purpose for

> *Each one of us needs to be consistently and continually reminded of God's redemption story.*

which He created us? The answer is simple. We can't and we won't. You may not own a hard copy of the Bible, or you may have five different translations of the Bible gathering dust on your bookshelf. Or you may have a Bible on your nightstand that has not been opened in weeks, months, or years. You know what? None of you are alone. My prayer for you and myself is that we will open the Bible this week and begin to fill our minds with God's Word. If you do not have a clue where to begin reading, I would suggest open up the Bible to the Gospel of John in the New Testament and simply start reading your heart out.

The more time we spend putting God's Word into our minds, the more His Word will become our thoughts. The more Scriptures we study, the more we will learn about our God's character. The more times we read through God's redemption story for His people, which is you and me, the more our hearts will humbly rejoice in the grace poured out upon our souls. The Lord has much work to do in our lives. He accomplishes this work through His Word, the working of His Holy Spirit, and the presence of other believers in our lives. The more time we spend reading about Jesus, the more we will view this life and all of this life's circumstances with the perspective that this place is not our forever home.

Sweet boys,

I pray in this moment that the Lord will overwhelm you with a desire for His Word, a curiosity to understand the Scriptures, the courage to ask questions when you read something you do not understand, and the faith that God's Word, which transcends all generations and all time, has the power to speak into your life. I pray, asking God to reveal Himself to you through the Bible. I pray the good news of Jesus Christ will transform your hearts and minds so that you begin to view this life through the lens of the gospel. My prayer for each of you is that reading the Bible will not be a legalistic task to complete but a form of worship that flows from a surrendered heart unto the Lord.

God's Word is a weapon, a powerful weapon, to use in our fight for holiness and our fight against the schemes of the evil one. Lord, may you sear your Word onto the hearts and into the minds of my boys.

my heart, mommy

Chapter 17

Keeping an Eternal Perspective

*"Therefore we do not give up. Even though our
outer person is being destroyed, our inner person is being
renewed day by day. For our momentary light affliction
is producing for us an absolutely incomparable eternal
weight of glory. So we do not focus on what is seen,
but on what is unseen. For what is seen is temporary,
but what is unseen is eternal."*
2 Corinthians 4:16–18

As I was driving to a women's event that our church was
hosting in October 2016, I experienced an all too jarringly
similar tightness in my chest. I once again felt the same
pressure collecting in my neck as I did on that Sunday
morning in December 2010. I was alone in the car and
driving on a highway. I had a silent debate between my

medical brain and my mommy heart for a few minutes as to whether or not these symptoms were, in fact, real. I glanced over at my purse, knowing the tiny bottle of nitroglycerin was tucked away in its safe home inside my wallet.

I tell myself over and over again it is not my job to self-diagnose. But I admit that this is oftentimes a challenge for me. As the pressure continued to build, the decision was obvious. I stuck the tiny pill under my tongue as I pulled into the parking lot and came to a stop. As I sat there in the driver's seat waiting to see if the pressure would lessen, I gazed up into the beautiful sun-setting sky and prayed, "God, I have no other choice but to trust You because Your Word displays Your trustworthiness."

To be clear, there is no way my initial response to potentially suffering a second heart attack would be this calm, this matter-of-fact, this accepting of whatever it is Jesus has for my life if I hadn't been spending time in the Word. Through more consistent reading and studying of the Bible prior to this moment, I learned more and more about the character of God and His amazing love for me and us as His children. Because of God's character and His love, I began to understand that I simply must trust and submit to His best plan for my life. As for tonight, if it ended with me making a visit to an emergency room, so be it.

I took a quick glance at my watch so I would know when to take the next tiny, dissolvable pill if my symptoms did not dissipate. I leaned my head back on the driver's seat headrest, closed my eyes, and waited. As I waited, I took slow, deep breaths in through my nose and exhaled slowly out of my mouth. It was only after six or seven breaths that I felt the nitroglycerin kicking in all over my body. In addition to the pressure in my chest and neck lessening, I felt the abrupt looseness of my blood vessels in my arms and legs. I continued sitting in the car for almost five more minutes before cautiously exiting and walking in the front doors of the evening gathering.

The room was dim with only candles and a few table lamps illuminating the space. As I took a few steps inward, I noticed that my friend and true kindred spirit, Rebecca, was walking straight toward me. We gave each other a hug, and with both an inquisitive and startled facial expression she said, "Julie, you are really warm." Because I know Rebecca and could say just about anything without her becoming rattled, I looked her directly in the eyes and without a hint of hesitation, I said, "Well, that is because I just took a nitroglycerin." She gave me *the* look. Before I knew it, I was sitting down in a comfortable chair and holding a bottle of water in my hand to replenish my fluids with hopes of counteracting my lowered blood pressure. Rebecca knows a thing or two about the medical world since she is a physical therapist. Plus, she has been at my bedside for every single one of my hospitalizations—from the heart-related admissions to the time my airway closed off. (Don't ask! I don't even know how that one happened. The emergency room physician was just as astounded.)

Rebecca has a gift of discerning needs of others without having to ask. Thus, she just sat with me and shared story after story so that all I needed to do was sit, rest, and listen (or pretend to listen). When I felt like I could respond without sensing any return of the chest pressure, I spoke up meekly, albeit with hesitation. The Lord used Rebecca in that moment not only to meet my physical needs by sitting me down and getting me water but also my emotional and spiritual needs through sharing God's Truth with me as we waited to see if the pressure in my neck and chest would return, offering up the opportunity for a girls' night out field trip to the emergency room.

God's sovereign hand kept the pain and the pressure at bay. He allowed this little episode to once again serve as a grace-filled reminder that today is a gift. The Lord provided a timely reminder, in Rebecca, to live with intentionality and purposefulness. This is what living in community is all about. When we both surround ourselves with other people that desire a life centered around Jesus and the gospel and allow these people into the vulnerable places of our hearts, we are reminded to live focused on the unseen—the promised—not the seen, which will waste away.

We need one another in this life. When our world feels like it is crumbling and there is no sight of daylight, we need our friends—our community—to pray and speak Truth over our lives. We need each other to display compassion and help with our physical, emotional, and spiritual needs. We need one another to serve as a safe place for confession. As we confess our sins and our struggles, we need one another to remind us of the gospel, which is that all of our sins are washed white as snow because of Christ's blood shed on the cross at Calvary.

Romans 8:1 tells us that there is no condemnation for those who are in Christ Jesus. What a gift it is for us to be accepted and loved by one another, not because we have perfect love for one another but because Christ the Lord has perfect love for us! I know it is risky. Believe me, I know. I know that being vulnerable is not easy or even simple. Opening up can

It is a gift for us to be accepted and loved by one another.

actually be quite messy . . . and it most likely will be. You are not alone in being scared or hesitant to reveal the deeper levels of yourself. Yet sometimes all it takes is one person taking the risk of opening up to create a safe place for others to be vulnerable.

I see this very thing played out in my friendships with three girls in particular. Once a week I meet up with these three ladies and we "go there." Yes, of course, we talk about our kids and what is going on in the outer layers of our onion-like lives. But then it only takes one of us to go deep by asking pointed questions for us to reveal what is at the core of our hearts. You might think that it is the same person every week that opens up and shares first. But that's not the case. You might think the same person week after week asks the purposeful

Christ the Lord has perfect love for us!

questions first. Not in our group. Regardless of who asks first or who answers first, the beautiful thing is that each one of us is committed to come to the table each week regardless of how we feel.

A few weeks ago I texted the girls to let them know I was feeling heavy from some of the burdens I felt myself carrying. As a result, I told them I sensed myself withdrawing and desiring isolation instead of community. Their response? They wouldn't let me withdraw! They would not allow me to rope myself off in the isolation room. Instead, they immediately texted Matthew 11:28–30: "Come to Me, all of you who are weary and burdened, and I will give you rest. All of you, take up My yoke and learn from Me, because I am gentle and humble in heart, and you will find rest for yourselves. For My yoke is easy and My burden is light." And Galatians 6:2: "Carry one another's burdens; in this way you will fulfill the law of Christ."

These girls, my people, slapped me in the face with God's Word. That made my heart and mind realize that I needed to take the focus off of myself and the weight of our circumstances and place my focus back on Jesus. I need community. We all need community. I want you to know that their pursuit of me did not end with these texts of Scripture. I received phone calls later in the day checking on me and received texts detailing how they were praying. Community is work. You should know that working for true community in your life is worth the mess, worth the fight, worth the sacrifice, and worth the inconvenience. At the end of the day, this life is about pursuing holiness and worshipping our Heavenly Father.

It is a refreshingly beautiful thing to watch our friendship grow deeper as we realize how weak and prone to wander each one of us is without Christ's constant pursuit of our hearts. Yes, our friendships grow deeper when there is vulnerability, confession, and the speaking of Scripture over one another's lives. Having community means much more than having mere lighthearted friendships. Biblical community is living with the goal of coming alongside one another and spurring one another on toward holiness. After all, isn't that why we were created? Scripture says we were created in the image of God so we would grow daily to look more and more like His character rather than the attributes and image of the world. True biblical community will not allow our hearts to wander without them pulling us back into the fight for holiness.

As Hebrews 10:23–25 says, "Let us hold on to the confession of our hope without wavering, for He who promised is faithful. And let us be concerned about one another in order to promote love and good works, not staying away from our worship meetings, as some habitually do, but encouraging each other, and all the more as you see the day drawing near." God uses this community, these friendships, over and over again in my life to refocus my eyes on Him in times when my eyes and heart shift away. When left to myself, I wander. I fall into self-pity. I seek fleeting satisfaction from the temporary and not fulfilling satisfaction in the eternal. Yes, God has certainly used community in my life in order for Him continually to win my heart's affections.

Living life surrounded by people that point us toward Jesus and consistently remind us of who we are in Christ is imperative. We need one another in this life because remaining steadfast and consistently grounded with an eternal perspective does not come easily. It actually comes with a lot of self-sacrifice. If maintaining an eternal perspective was easy, then maybe we might glance through any location where crowds form and actually see people engaging with one another more than they engage with their iPhones. Sadly, I keep seeing more and more people distracted by frivolous things on this earth that truly have little to no eternal significance. And it really does sadden me. I wish people would value *real* community over virtual community.

> *Remaining steadfast and consistently grounded with an eternal perspective does not come easily.*

John and I work hard to leave our cell phones by our car keys in the evenings. Our desire is to be disconnected from the world (if only for a couple of hours) where there is an unspoken pressure that every text message must receive an immediate response. This doesn't always happen, and I confess that it somehow takes a lot of mental energy to leave the phone on the counter. However, we are earnestly making this choice because John and I both desire for our three boys to grow up knowing without a shadow of doubt where our affections fall: on Jesus, on our marriage, and on them. Not stuff. Not information. Not work. Not baseball scores and stats. Not Instagram. Not Twitter. Not Pinterest. But *their* souls.

Boys,

I love you. Every night when you lay your head on your pillow to sleep, I beg the Lord to awaken your spirit to love Him and serve Him with your lives. I desire nothing more for your life than for you to have an enduring faith in Jesus. Although I strive to display Jesus in my own life, I am not perfect. In fact,

I make mistakes all the time. You are aware of my mistakes and the countless times I have needed to confess my wrongs to you and ask for forgiveness. And, even though I too often fail, Jesus never fails. Praise be to the Lord for His promise in Romans 8:38–39, which shares that nothing can separate us from the love of God. Living this life for Jesus will be met with resistance from the world. But the world has no say over the God of all creation. God desires our affections, and He desires for us to live with an eternal perspective.

Even now I am praying for the Lord to bring mentors and accountability into your lives. I know a day will come—all too soon approach—when you will no longer desire to spend every waking moment with Mommy and Daddy. I pray for God-fearing men that will invest in your lives. I pray for men that would serve as role models in your life and consistently remind you of the gospel. I pray you will bravely take the risk of allowing others to know you. Boys, we are not supposed to live this life as if it were an individual sport. No. This life is meant to be lived in true, biblical community. You need real, authentic friends to be your teammates who will encourage you as you press on toward eternity in glory.

I pray now that the Lord will provide true friends in your lives who also desire to live authentically for Christ, who also long for holiness, who also value the importance of confessing sin and receiving forgiveness from the Lord that is possible because of Christ's death on the cross and resurrection from the grave. There will be friendships in your life that will remain at a surface level. This is to be expected. But the Bible is clear that we are to live deeply, confessing our sins with one another, that we ought to be known—the good, the bad, and the ugly—so that we might encourage, rebuke, and guide one another on in this race we are to run this side of heaven. I pray fervently that you will learn from an early age the importance of not hiding your sin but rather confessing your sin to others. Trust that you will experience freedom through confession. I pray you will learn how to be vulnerable within a small group of friends with whom to share your struggles, victories, and dreams.

I love you so deeply.

my heart, mommy

Chapter 18

Who Do I Believe I Am?

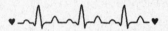

> *"Look at how great a love the Father has given us
> that we should be called God's children. And we are!"*
> 1 JOHN 3:1

Looking back over the past five years, I have done my best to live intentionally—present and focused on the moment at hand.

Recently John and I vacationed in Mexico with another couple and their two boys. This couple is special to us. Ryan is both a significant encouragement to John in the faith and a coworker. Ryan and his wife, Jenna, are the type of friends with whom vulnerability comes naturally. While in Mexico, John and I joked with Ryan that when planning this trip, we didn't realize a chef was part of the package. Ryan has a true love for grilling and preparing food. So each evening he led and directed the team in the kitchen. I do not mind one bit being assigned a task. In fact, I really like it when I am assigned a task to complete. Chalk that up to my desire to feel productive. Ha! And I also enjoy cooking in the kitchen. That is, when I am not carrying the stress of perfectly timing each dish's completion so that everything is served at its ideal temperature. If you are a kitchen professional, you may be rolling your eyes and calling me an amateur. For the rest of us, at least one part of dinner has to be reheated in the microwave because something else took too long to prepare.

One evening in Mexico I was not needed in the kitchen. Instead, John and I sat out on the porch with our boys. Hearing the music from the speakers, Hunter sweetly asked me if I would dance with him. Oh, my heart just leaped with joy! He grabbed my hand as I stood up from my chair and led me to the patio near the swimming pool. I placed his right hand on my hip and took his left hand in mine, and we began to sway side to side, stepping ever so slightly. Just close your eyes and remember those sixth-grade dances, and you'll have a good idea of what we looked like. Just as girls lead the dancing in middle school, tonight with Hunter would be no different. Every thirty seconds or so, Hunter would spin himself in a circle. After his first spin he said, "Mommy, I'm sorry, but I am just not tall enough yet to twirl you like Daddy twirls you." Melt my heart. As the song concluded, he motioned for me to lean down toward him, and he planted a sweet kiss on my cheek.

Hunter is a freshly turned six-year-old now, but I can already envision him being the little boy who has all the girls chasing him around the playground. I am just going to apologize right now for all the hearts this little boy might break in his lifetime! Noah, however, is coming into the age of self-awareness. It took three songs and some intense coaxing by John to convince him to ask me to dance. While Hunter was excited to dance with Mommy, Noah vacillated between, "I love my Mom, but this is kind of awkward and embarrassing." Yet all I could think about on this overcast, eerily cool and breezy evening in Mexico was how much I absolutely love my boys and how this is going to be one of those memories I will recall if I am still around to witness them marry the girls that win their hearts.

I truly desire to make memories with my children. But not only do I want to make memories; I desire to actually *remember* these memories, and I want my children to remember these moments, too. I journal about our first dances, the silly things they say, the stroller rides, and the times they spook me so badly that I scream and they laugh hysterically. (Thank you, John, for instigating the *spooking of Mommy*.) I also journal about the character they are building as they learn more about Jesus.

I want life to be filled with intentional memory making. I do not want to live life anxiously waiting for the next season when babies finally sleep through the night or fit-throwing toddlers transform into four-year-old helpers. Let me not wish for the day when the youngest begins kindergarten because that will be the day my oldest begins middle school. Then I will blink, and we will be taking kids to college. No! I do not want to rush life. I want to embrace as much eye contact as my kids will give me. I want to facilitate conversations as we drive through traffic headed toward baseball practice and as we sit around the dinner table. I want to take moments to dance with my boys on the porch.

Why is this? Why do I want to press pause? Is it because life seems to be going by more swiftly now than it did when I was in high school? Is it because I live with a chronic illness and because I have been told I am at risk to die suddenly? No. I do not just want my boys to know me and remember me when I am gone. Of course I want to leave a legacy of service, love, and generosity. But what good is my legacy if they do not know and love the Giver of life? No. I desire to show them Jesus. Jesus was an intentional memory maker. Jesus was always fully present. He did not live a life of distraction. He did not live a life with selfish ambition. Jesus was purposeful in conversation, purposeful in His actions, and purposeful in embracing every moment. Jesus knew the cross was coming.

> *Jesus was purposeful in conversation, purposeful in His actions, and purposeful in embracing every moment. Jesus knew the cross was coming.*

He knew from day one the purpose of His life would entail persecution, sacrifice, and ultimate death upon the cross to be the propitiation for the sins of all, once and for all.

What would it look like if women around the world started to put down their iPhones and spent less time scrolling through apps? What if women spent more time looking into the eyes of people around them and had conversations about Jesus, reading through the Bible together and praying to the One who is worthy above all else? What if lunch notes, texts, and cards stopped saying, "Have a great day!" and instead included a prayer over their soul and a Scripture to cling to that is Truth as they decipher through the lies heard in the hallways, on the sidewalks, or next to the water cooler? What if we chased our children around the park and on the way home tell them that Jesus is chasing after them, and He never runs out of breath like Mommy? What if we stopped calling our minivan a taxi and begin seeing the opportunity for discipleship of the souls that are buckled into their seats with no place else to go? What if we actually shared the gospel with our children instead of rushing them through life? What if we stop playing church like we played house as children and actually started being the church?

May we turn into a generation of women who live with constant intentionality. Not just for the sake of being intentional but for the sake of living like Christ. May we also be a generation of women who dares to dream of how God might just use our lives tomorrow while we are in the trenches of today.

I remember running into Jennie at a Christmas gathering nearly one year to the day after suffering the heart attack at church. I did not have the pleasure of knowing Jennie prior to the birth of Hunter. So she did not know "pre-heart failure Julie." She did not know the career-driven, ambitious, knowledge-seeking, competitive Julie.

Regardless of the fact that our friendship was on the newer side, our conversation skipped right over the surface and went straight to the deep end of the pool. From that moment I knew Jennie and I would be friends and not just acquaintances. Despite being surrounded by people in a crowded space, our conversation felt as if we were the only two in the room. Somewhere in the middle of our conversation and even somewhat disconnected from our conversation topic, she very frankly asked, "So, Julie, do you even allow yourself to think about next year or the next few years?" I felt my heart sink into my chest and somewhat sadly answered, "No. I am having trouble looking past this evening, let alone next week."

Recounting this conversation is somewhat challenging because it promptly reminds that I used to be *"that girl."* I was the girl who once had her one-year, five-year, and ten-year goals written down and saved in a document on the computer to be reviewed throughout the year. Somehow now I found my diagnosis defining my identity and impacting my ability to dream. At some point I simply stopped dreaming. At some point I did not feel as if I could dream. My diagnosis paralyzed me. I was allowing my circumstances to be my identity instead of believing who God says I am in His Word. His Word states in Genesis 1 that we are created in the image of God. First John 3:1 states, "Look at how great a love the Father has given us that we should be called God's children. And we are!" Each one of us is fearfully and wonderfully made (Ps. 139), and we are His beloved daughters. This is what defines us—not our circumstances.

This conversation with Jennie filtered through my thoughts from time to time over the next few years. But I never spent the time to process the idea of dreaming up long-term plans for my life. I had allocated all of my bandwidth to only those things that were within my arms' reach. Yet in recent months I have come to realize that I was stuck and, if I am being completely transparent, somewhat scared to become unstuck. I was living with such a degree of nearsightedness that I began having difficulty making decisions about things that would happen the following day or the following week. Part of me had been on "lockdown." The part that really enjoyed dreaming and goal setting. And my heart was being convicted that if the Lord gives me just one more year or even another twenty years here on the earth, I do not want to grow stagnant and complacent and cease growing as a woman of faith.

When John first asked me out on a date, I said no. Ouch! Well, not exactly. I actually awkwardly asked him for a "rain check." Yes, I really did say "rain check." How awful, right?! I crushed his spirit, and yet he stood there with a smile on his face. Prior to knowing John, I had experienced a severely broken heart and had built up thick, impenetrable walls around myself. In that moment I could not allow any potential threat to climb over the wall and into my heart. Not even the potential for someone to love me. Well, this same type of guardedness had slowly crept back into my life. It was not guardedness against loving others or receiving love, for I desired and still desire for everyone in my life to know how much I value and love them. No, this was guardedness against dreaming. Hidden beneath this guardedness is my fear that I may not be able to experience this dream or desire due to a shortened life on this earth. So, "Julie logic," as John likes to call it, told my heart to stop dreaming. This solution would eliminate the potential threat of hurt. Both the hurt within my own heart and the hurt that could be caused to my children if Mommy does not get to accomplish those dreams alongside them.

Okay, so let's just call it like it is. This is not Truth. Jesus is better than any dream I could ever dream or anything I could accomplish this side of heaven. Jesus will use all things for good. Can you tell that Romans 8:28 has become my war cry? Yes, absolutely, there will be dreams my children have that my eyes will never see. And, you know what? Jesus will pursue after them in those moments of sadness, disappointment, or even frustration. Jesus will show Himself as *enough* for them. Because, after all, my children's identity is not that they are children of a chronically ill mommy. Rather, they are, like us, created in God's image, fearfully and wonderfully made, and called children of the King of kings who really does sit on a throne in the heavenlies that our eyes will see face-to-face one day. If we could just hammer this Truth into our heads long and hard enough for belief to take root, then maybe our battle with our fears would lessen over time. Jesus, will You forgive my unbelief?! Jesus, will You birth FAITH within my

> *Jesus is better than any dream I could ever dream or anything I could accomplish this side of heaven.*

soul! Will you replace the fear or anxiety or lack of belief in each one of our lives with faith in You and Your Word?

I have just recently started to dream again. The risk of disappointment is real. I am dreaming of being used by Jesus not only today but also tomorrow and next month. I am dreaming, asking, and praying for God to reveal what His hand is calling us toward as a family. My fear in living only in the nearsightedness is that I will look up six months from now and not have changed or grown or moved forward in my walk with Christ. Thus, I need some measure of ebb and flow between the near and the farsightedness. But how? Is a formula available? Can I execute some perfect plan? God penned the Scripture in Psalm 46:10 to help us answer these questions, "Be still, and know that I am God" (NIV). In the stillness we sense the Holy Spirit. Sensing the Holy Spirit's nudging of our souls through reading the Bible consistently and praying often is the catalyst that allows our lives to reflect the glory and redemption of the cross in this moment and the moment to follow.

Sweet boys,

I am so thankful for each one of your lives. Each one of you has a drive to succeed and an innate desire to work hard. God created you to be men, men of godly character. He created you to work. I hope and pray that as you grow in maturity, you will also cling to what God says is your identity. You are His. You are His children. You are a new creation because of Christ. You are created in His image. Yes, you may become a doctor or an engineer or a fireman or even a "ninja in space" one day. But, know that your identity, the identity that is found in Christ, the identity that the Lord of all creation gave to you does not change regardless of your profession, your successes, or your failures. When we are secure in our identity as loved children of God, no matter what circumstances we face, we can fall on our knees in prayer, confident as His children that He will listen to our voices and direct our steps. Never be afraid to dream big dreams with the Lord. He will catch you if you fall, and He will make His name great through your life. Your worth, your value is found in Christ and Christ alone. I love you.

my heart, mommy

Chapter 19

Whose Voice Am I Listening To?

"But from there, you will search for the LORD your God, and you will find Him when you seek Him with all your heart and all your soul."
DEUTERONOMY 4:29

Hunter was two years old when I began to truly process through the reality that physically carrying more children in my womb was not an option. John and I were initially told this news when Hunter was less than eight weeks of age. Let's be honest, not only was I sleep deprived from having a newborn and exhausted from watching my twenty-month-old run circles around the house, but my every drop of energy was focused and determined on merely staying alive. My longing and desires were to live long enough to

watch my children grow up and go off to kindergarten. The
topic of expanding our family at that point in time was not
even on my radar. It was not on the map.

Yet, as Hunter was entering the *terrific* twos, I was
blindsided with sadness each month. This would have
been the season where we would have tried to get pregnant
had our circumstances been different. Prior to marriage,
John and I discussed our thoughts on how many children
we envisioned raising. I giggle as I remember John clearly
desiring three children while I would typically respond
with a wink, "Why don't we just take things one child at
a time." John and I believe what Psalm 127:3–5 states is
true, "Sons are indeed a heritage from the LORD, children,
a reward. Like arrows in the hand of a warrior are the sons
born in one's youth. Happy is the man who has filled his
quiver with them." Yes, our quiver had two fiery, energetic
boys bouncing around inside of it. And here I was, two
years later, facing another reality, another "new normal"
that I had been suppressing. In my stubbornness—yes, I
am confessing my stubborn heart—I wanted to revisit the
topic of future pregnancies with a physician who special-
izes in the care of women who endure high-risk pregnancies. I had a sliver of unjustified hope that maybe, just
maybe, for some crazy reason the medical world might
change its mind and give John and me the "green light" to
keep having babies.

John, in his compassion and love, agreed to make
the appointment. Although John already anticipated the
outcome of the discussion. After all, my cardiologist had
already said, "No." My OB/Gyn had already said, "No."
And all my colleagues in pediatric cardiology had said,

"No." Yet John knew my emotional heart needed to gather more information to fully process what I was told during Hunter's infancy. I can still hear the doctor's words as clear as day. Although her voice conveyed sorrow, her words were anything but comforting to the heart: "Julie, your heart function has not fully recovered over the past three years. You are still reliant on medication to support your heart muscle. Even if you had fully recovered, you would be up against a 15 percent mortality rate during pregnancy alone. Yet, in your case, you are looking at a 50 percent chance of not surviving the pregnancy and nearly full assurance of the progression of your heart failure." This response was not what I wanted to hear. I felt as if another dream was stomped upon. And, frankly, I was tired of being stomped on.

As John and I somberly left that appointment hand in hand, not a word was spoken as we quietly walked through the crowded waiting room full of pregnant women. Even as we walked through the fluorescent-lit hallway in search of the elevator, not a word slipped out from our mouths . . . although my heart must have left a mess on the floor leaving a path for all to find. I felt the weight of the tears welling up in my eyes as the elevator rhythmically lowered one floor at a time transporting us to the lobby of the building. As we exited the building, it was there that words finally broke the silence. With an aching heart I passionately proclaimed, "But, my God is bigger than statistics!" In the middle of the parking lot, John turned toward me, wrapped his arms around me—holding the back of my head with one hand and embracing my back with the other—and calmly responded, "Julie, you are right. God is bigger. Julie, the answer is easy for me. Noah and Hunter need their mommy, and I need my wife." John tenderly affirmed me in that moment saying that the Lord had given us the blessing of Noah and Hunter, and the Lord is asking us to trust Him with our family.

John was so gentle in his words and so accepting of our situation. He was content with our family of four and expressed how overly blessed he was with being the daddy of Noah and the daddy of Hunter. Sure, John would love to raise a basketball team of boys, but he was satisfied with what God had given to us. The two boys the Lord created to be our sons.

I was the one who needed to confess my desires to the Lord and wait for God to both soften my heart to His plan and to move my heart from being in a state of *want* to being in a state of *thankfulness* for that which I was given. And He did. God was faithful to soften my heart to a place of surrender to His plan. Over the ensuing months friends of ours gave birth to new babies, and other friends were traveling across the globe to bring home their children through adoption. The sting of watching pregnant bellies growing bigger and then watching the miracle of life take its first breaths slowly faded. My heart sincerely rejoiced as I watched the Lord

> *I am thankful for the thorn in my flesh—the thorn that keeps my eyes on my Big God rather than on tiny me.*

continue to fill others' quivers with even more arrows. Even so I was reminded of the thorn in my flesh, the thorn that keeps my eyes on my big God rather than on tiny me.

I prayed. I poured my heart out to the Lord. And I prayed more and more until the Lord shifted my heart to say, "It is well with my soul."

One year later, in the fall of 2012, our pastors preached through a sermon series on how God accomplishes more through the gospel than simply forgiveness for those who believe. Through the gospel, followers of Jesus Christ are adopted as sons and daughters into the family of God. Because we are sons and daughters of the living God, this changes how we live life this side of heaven. The sermon series also examined our call as the church to care for the orphan. I confess, John and I did not leave church after those three Sundays and immediately feel led to pursue adoption. But we were convicted to start praying and began asking the Lord to help us discern in what capacity our family would love on and care for the orphan. And so we prayed.

As months passed and we continued to pray, one thing was clear: neither John nor I was opposed to our family growing through adoption. Not one bit. In fact, it was quite the opposite. The more we grew to see and love how adoption beautifully displays the gospel, the more our hearts grew unified that adoption was not an *if* but a *when*. And the *when* discussion caused our hearts to pray to the Lord for discernment. We sought counsel from friends who had walked the adoption path before us who encouraged us to pray, asking the Lord to draw our hearts to unity and cause our motivations to be pure. After all, if we were going to pursue adoption, it was not going to be simply because we wanted to get another buddy for our boys. Rather, if we were going to pursue a third son, it was going to be because we both felt convicted that we were to disciple another soul.

Nearly nine months later John and I started our adoption journey. Over the long season of prayer, the Lord brought our hearts to a unified place where John and I were both excited *at the same time* to learn more about a few potential adoption agencies and locate a social worker to complete a home study for us. Our hearts were ready to tackle the mound of required paperwork. Knowing that our desire was to pursue a domestic adoption, I began making phone calls to various agencies and social workers recommended to us by families we knew that had also adopted domestically.

I remember sitting in my car in Home Depot's parking lot when one of the social workers returned my call. From conversations with others, I knew this particular social worker was a "tough cookie" and yet an invaluable resource through her decades of experience. With that said, I was not expecting to hear much compassion or fluff in her words. She was, however, extremely kind and patient to listen to our family's story. After speaking for approximately ten minutes, I asked, "How would you guide our family in pursuing this adoption?"

I had prepared myself for all of the colorful responses she might give to our family *except* for the actual one response she did offer. "Julie, from what you just shared with me, I do not believe you are actually a candidate for adoption. I do not know of any agencies in town or around the state that would be willing to accept you given your health history. Additionally, I am not sure that any birth mother would be open to accepting you either."

I could NOT have seen this coming. I was devastated. I felt as if I had suddenly gotten the wind knocked out of me. It was such a range of emotions. My heart journeyed from hope and excitement at one end of the pendulum to being thrown onto the floor smashing into hundreds of pieces all within minutes as I closed the conversation with, "Thank you for spending this time to speak with me."

My initial thoughts were of self-pity. Not only was I told I could not birth any more children, but now I was being told that I could not even adopt a child. Stunned and confused, I could not even pick up the phone to call John and share how the last fifteen minutes of my life had swung so quickly from one end of the spectrum to the other. I simply sat in that same Home Depot parking spot and cried out to God. "John and I have peace that pursuing adoption was to be our family's story. Why are we being shut down? Lord, are we somehow missing something? Did we miss Your discernment on this? Are we wrong? Are You not asking us to adopt? Are we pursuing this adoption with a heart of selfishness rather than with a heart of obedience? I'm so confused."

As other adoption agencies and social workers returned my phone calls, we sadly heard a common theme . . . because of my heart issues, adoption was going to be challenging . . . and it might not happen at all. I felt somewhat paralyzed by the words of rejection that seemed to come rather consistently from so many unconnected sources.

Several weeks after having all of these conversations, I remember coming home from the grocery store. Noah and Hunter were both in school. Right there, in the rare silence of our home and in the middle of putting away food in the pantry, I sensed in my heart a heavy conviction from the Holy Spirit. I sensed that the God of the universe wanted to know whose voice was valued most in my life. Was His voice enough? Or would I continue to bounce between His voice and the voices of the world. The voices are different from one another. The world says, "When things get tough, give up." God says, "I will endure you, and I will move you to where I want you to be." The world says, "Make much of your own name." God says, "I will make much of My own name." God's name is the name above ALL names. No name is greater than that of God Almighty. The world says, "Store up for yourself treasure on this earth." God says, "Store up your treasure in heaven where moth and rust do not destroy" (see Matt. 6:19–20). The world says, "Every day should be exciting and adventurous, filled with passions and fulfillment." God says, "I alone fully satisfy." God moves mightily in the routine and mundane of everyday. The world says, "walk in the path of least resistance." God says, "The road is narrow which leads to life."

> *The world says, "When things get tough, give up." God says, "I will endure you, and I will move you to where I want you to be."*

The world was telling us no to adoption. But God. The God that is bigger than statistics. The God that performs miracles. The God that asks each of us to take risks, believing that He is always with us and will catch us when we fall. The God that is in control of all things. *My* God was already working in the heart of the woman He would use to bring our son home to our family.

Boys,

My hope is that you will know that the Lord is at work even in the midst of what feels like silence, rejection, and adversity. He is at work even when obstacles seem to block the path you've believed He is directing you toward. Sometimes God will test your faithfulness. He will examine your heart to determine if you value His voice or the voice of this world. He does this because He desires all of you. All of your affections, not just a portion of them.

God is the same yesterday, today, and tomorrow. You can trust His Word. You can trust His character. And you can trust the Holy Spirit working in and through your life. He will always direct your steps in this life. He knows your heart, and He knows the best path for your life.

You are loved.

my heart, mommy

Chapter 20

Love Beyond Words

"Every good thing given and every perfect gift is from above, coming down from the Father of lights, with whom there is no variation or shifting shadow."
JAMES 1:17 (NASB)

Ms. Charlotte is hands down one of the most amazing, compassionate, loving, advocating, prayerful, and Spirit-filled women ever to enter into our family's life. Many years ago the Lord developed within Ms. Charlotte a passion to come alongside birth mothers, speaking wisdom and truth into their lives as they walk the road of adoption. Ms. Charlotte also prayerfully searches for adoptive families with whom to place these precious children. A friend of ours had known Ms. Charlotte for several years and asked if John and I would mind if she shared our story with her. Well, of course I wanted our friend, Natalie, to share our story. At the same time, I was nervous that we would, once again, face the same words of discouragement and rejection we heard two months earlier. I sensed my heart rebuilding walls around it, as if the walls could actually protect me from disappointment. Despite my fears, Natalie made the phone call on our behalf. I found myself needing to trust God. Even if we faced another rejection, He would be enough to bind up those wounds.

A few days later my cell phone rang late in the evening. Bedtime stories had been read, Noah and Hunter were tucked into their beds, and in that moment I was in the process of folding one last load of laundry. I did not recognize the number on my phone and almost didn't answer. To my surprise it was not a wrong number. Instead, I heard the most gentle-spirited voice on the other end of the line. It was Ms. Charlotte. She began sharing with me about her conversation with Natalie and the conviction that her own heart had experienced, prompting her to make this phone call. Simply put, Ms. Charlotte wanted to help John and me find our son. I was without words. I had grown to expect another no, another shut door, another rejection. And yet, in that moment, I was so overwhelmed with the kindness of the Lord and simultaneously filled with such nervous excitement that I could hardly sleep.

> *Even if we faced another rejection, He would be enough to bind up those wounds.*

It was a typical Sunday, really. Our home study was scheduled for the upcoming week. We had taken the boys to church and then headed to one of the boys' favorite lunch spots. On the way home, we chatted about the anticipated lazy afternoon of watching football and playing our new favorite game with the boys called "cards and marbles." John pulled in the driveway and passed me the house key so I could get the door unlocked while he unloaded the boys from the backseat.

As I approached, I could hear a very loud noise coming from inside the house. A noise that became exponentially louder as I opened the door. I only took a few steps inside before I started screaming. With each successive step I screamed again and again. I rushed through the dining room to the front entryway to view water flowing down our stairs with the force of a rumbling stream. Water was falling from every air vent and light fixture. Ceilings were buckling from the weight of the water coming from the second floor and shortly thereafter gave way, falling down on our furniture in the living room and office.

John and I both went sprinting up the stairs to find the source of the water, not even thinking that we could potentially fall through to the floor below. Thankfully, we did find the busted toilet pipe and were able to turn the water off, but we were unable to keep our home from being completely and utterly destroyed. Within the next twenty-four hours, our home was ripped apart all the way down to the studs and foundation, and most of our belongings were ruined.

Needless to say, we had to cancel our home study since we technically no longer had a home. I just kept thinking to myself that something or someone was trying anything and everything to keep us from adopting. The enemy attempted to use our circumstances to shake us, but, as believers, we do not stand on shifting ground. Rather, we stand upon the Rock; thus, we will not be shaken. Even though the waters raged and destroyed our physical home. Even though I live with a defibrillator in my chest. Our God is still on His throne, and nothing can thwart His plan for our lives.

> *We stand upon the Rock; thus, we will not be shaken. Though the waters rage, our God is still on His throne, and nothing can thwart His plan for our lives.*

I am reminded of James 1:2–4, which states: "Consider it a great joy, my brothers, whenever you experience various trials, knowing that the testing of your faith produces endurance. But endurance must do its complete work, so that you may be mature and complete, lacking nothing." Instead of doubting our steps, John and I became determined to persevere in the calling to adopt. Our passion grew even more fierce to find the little one we could call son. And so we did just that. We spent the next few weeks bunking up with a dear, sweet family from the boys' school as we searched for a more long-term housing plan. As we settled into an apartment, we completed our adoption paperwork and even had our home study performed so we would be ready whenever we received *the* phone call from Charlotte telling us to come meet our newborn baby boy.

It was another beautiful Sunday about eight months later. We'd been back in our renovated home for only a few weeks. Once again John and I took the boys to their same favorite lunch spot after church. On our car ride home from lunch, John and I discussed what fun things we wanted to do with Noah and Hunter over the last two weeks of summer vacation. Would we make one more trip up to Dallas to visit my parents? Would we drive up to Fort Worth to visit some dear friends? Our two boys were getting a little restless hanging out with Mommy all day. Suddenly, I was no longer as fun to them as I had been just weeks earlier. Shooting baskets in the backyard and riding their bikes up and down the street for hours was fun in June, but these things had lost their luster by August. I admit, I had exhausted all of my creative juices coming up with fun summer activities, and evidently this mental exhaustion carried over into my ability to be decisive. After an hour of conversation that hot August afternoon, John and I still did not have a plan. I told John that maybe a short walk would help me clear my mind, so I laced up my tennis shoes, grabbed a bottle of water, and headed out the door. My phone started ringing as I was walking down our driveway. I was not going to answer it, but then I thought it might be John needing something. So I pulled the phone out of my pocket. John's number was not on the caller ID. It was Ms. Charlotte.

It. Was. Charlotte!!!

I frantically answered for fear that I had already allowed my phone to ring too long and hoped I could catch her before she landed in my voicemail. My voice went nearly one octave higher, "Hi Ms. Charlotte!!"

She somewhat chuckled at my hello and then said, "Well, hi Julie. I have some news. Is now a good time to talk?"

"Yes! Of course! Of course this is a good time!" I replied. As I made the trek back up our long, steep driveway, I listened to Ms. Charlotte skip right over the small talk and begin sharing the news.

There was a baby. The tiny baby boy had been born in the wee hours of that Sunday morning. When I say "tiny," I mean tiny—four pounds, five ounces of tiny—and just shy of two months early. Because his birth mother went into preterm labor, she had not yet had a chance to meet with Charlotte to select an adoptive family, and now Ms. Charlotte anxiously wanted to know if John and I would be interested in having our family considered by the birth mommy.

My reply was, "Yes, yes. Absolutely! YES!"

At this point John was peering at me through the kitchen window with bewilderment as to why I was pacing around in circles underneath our carport. After all, I had left to go on a walk nearly fifteen minutes earlier. John's curiosity pulled him outside to join me. He attempted to ask me who was on the other line, but I just kept my eyes to the ground and handed him the sheet of paper I was writing on. I circled three words for his eyes to see: "Charlotte," "Boy," "NICU." You should have seen the grin on his face! It was the same grin he had when I told him that I was pregnant with Noah. A few moments later we wrapped up our phone call, and Charlotte said she would get back to us once the little one's birth mommy had made a decision.

I had plans to go out with a few girlfriends that night to celebrate my birthday. We went to a painting class where an instructor guides the class step-by-step through painting a selected scene. Somehow, despite everyone's artistic ability or lack thereof, each painting turns out impressively and uniquely well done. All of us were in the middle of painting dabs of leaves on a tree's branches when my cell phone started ringing. I hurriedly answered as I continued to paint. It was Charlotte.

My sweet friend, Jenna, started noticing that the rate and size for which I was painting leaves dramatically increased as I listened to Charlotte speak. Jenna snatched the paintbrush from my hand nearly midstroke and motioned for me to go outside. As she smiled from ear to ear, she said, "I can *fix* your leaves!" Evidently I went a little too crazy with my leaf painting! As I stepped outside onto the sidewalk, Charlotte joyously shared that the precious birth mommy had chosen us to be the little boy's parents. She had chosen Noah and Hunter to be his big brothers. In a matter of what felt like minutes, John and I went from planning out the final two weeks of summer to having a baby!

I was over the moon with joy. I raced back inside to share the news with the girls. Another friend asked, "What did John say?!" Well, let's just say that I immediately did an about-face and ran back outside to make the phone call to Johnny. And we were over the moon together.

Two years of deciding to pursue adoption and eight months of waiting, wondering, and hoping for a baby boy were not without moments of fear and doubt creeping back in. I mean, literally just twenty-four hours prior to answering the phone call from Charlotte, I found myself in a conversation with the Lord asking Him if He was even in our situation. I asked the Lord to search my heart and show me if John and I were pursuing adoption with a selfish ambition or if He was truly the author of our desires.

That Saturday, merely hours before Joshua was born, John and I spent the day with two other couples at a lake house just outside of town. After a late lunch we made our way to the boat dock to cruise around the lake in the ski boat. As I glanced out on the water, I talked with the Lord about my fears and doubts and uncertainty. Would we ever have a third child? I nearly started crying as I poured out my heart to Him. I moved my gaze from the lake waters to the back of the boat where John was sitting and talking with one of the other husbands. And right there for my eyes to see was a rainbow. A rainbow that went from one side of the boat to the other. And I was overcome by the kindness of the Lord. Not because the rainbow was confirmation that John and I were rightly pursuing the path of adoption. Rather, the rainbow reminded me that God is God. The rainbow reminded me that God's Word can be trusted. The rainbow reminded me that God keeps His promises. The rainbow reminded me that God is trustworthy and true. Being reminded of God's character in that moment brought me peace in our waiting. Once we returned to the boat dock, I shared with the other gals the conversation I was having with the Lord and of the rainbow my eyes saw resting just over the heads of our husbands. When I texted these ladies less than twenty-four hours later to share that our little boy had been born, they were quick to remind me of this rainbow and of God's character!

The Lord was so sweet to give us little Joshua, the boy we fervently pray will be "strong and courageous." Joshua spent three weeks in the NICU, and the Lord was so gracious to give me that time with him in the hospital. The first time John and I laid eyes on Joshua, you could hardly see his face because of all the tubes and equipment attached to him supporting his tiny body as it adjusted to life outside the womb. But he was certainly a cute little guy. Yes, he was tiny, but I could tell that he was a fighter. Five days out of the week, I would sit with Joshua for twelve-plus hours a day. I initially cared for him just as I would for any of my patients in the intensive care unit. But day after day something was changing. My affections grew more and more in love with him. I went from being his nurse who fed him and rotated his position in his warming crib to feeling guilty for leaving him to head back to Austin for a day or two to love on Noah and Hunter. By the time I needed to make my third short trip back home, I whispered to Joshua that next time I came back to the NICU, Mommy would not be able to leave without him. My heart would not be able to bear it.

I have a journal for each one of our three boys that contain letters I have written to each of them over the last few years. On August 9, 2014, I wrote this letter to Joshua in his journal:

Joshua,

Daddy and I have prayed for you for nearly two and a half years. The Lord put you in our hearts before He even created you. And, though there were years drawing our hearts to you, you came into our lives so very unexpectedly.

You need to know how loved you are. You are loved by Jesus. You are loved by Mommy and Daddy and Noah and Hunter. You are loved by your sweet "tummy" mommy who gave you a warm and nurturing home in her belly so that you could grow and develop. Your birth mommy is a strong and courageous mommy, full of overflowing love for you.

We named you Joshua because the Lord commanded Joshua in the Bible to be strong and courageous time and time again. Joshua was brave and faithful. Joshua took risks, believing that God was always on his side. This is Mommy and Daddy's prayer for your life. We pray that you will be faithfully strong and courageous, taking risks for the sake of sharing Jesus with others.

"Joshua" means "the Lord saves." It is not Mommy and Daddy that save your soul. The Lord Almighty alone saves, and we pray that you will grow to know and love the Lord with all your heart, mind, soul, and strength.

*I cannot wait for you to meet your two big brothers. They are spending time with Nana and Papa while I am here with you in the hospital. They talk about you **all** the time, and* *they are very concerned about your stinky diapers! (As all little boys are!)*

You are precious, Joshua. I love you. I truly love you!

my heart, mommy

Boys,

I want to tell you what an honor it is to be your mother. The three of you teach me so much every day. Noah and Hunter, the love birthed in your hearts for Joshua is so full, so beautiful, so innate. The amount of excitement and joy and pride you take in having Joshua as your brother could not have been scripted any more beautifully. Your eyes and your hearts see your brother and not a different DNA. I know I have written to you much about enduring and persevering through the hard circumstances of life. But I also desire for you to know that taking time to pause . . . to sit still in the midst of persevering . . . and praise the Lord for the small, the big, and even the tiniest of tiny blessings will keep you rooted in Him from whom all blessings flow.

A mother's love is so complex and deep. I love you boys so much—so much it really does begin to hurt if I spend much time dwelling on it. I want to protect you. I want to guide you. I want to set you up for success and yet teach you how to come out on the other side of failure with more strength and character. I want you to know the depths of my love for you.

I want you to know me. And yet, at the end of my very long list of "I wants" for your life, I end up in a place of desperation before the throne of God as I sneak into your bedroom at night to check on you one more time before I lay my head on my own pillow. There is something so incredibly peaceful about you boys as you sleep. I watch you rest in complete surrender and trust that Jesus will cause your bodies to breathe and your hearts to beat. In those moments my eyes grow wet as I beg Jesus to awaken each one of your souls to love Him and trust Him and believe that He is enough for your little lives that will one day grow and develop into big lives. I pray that each one of you boys will live for the sole purpose of serving Jesus with every breath. I want you to know, realize, and live displaying belief that Jesus is worth everything and from Him comes every blessing.

my heart, mommy

Chapter 21

Finish Strong

"Therefore, since we also have such a large cloud of witnesses surrounding us, let us lay aside every weight and the sin that so easily ensnares us. Let us run with endurance the race that lies before us, keeping our eyes on Jesus, the source and perfecter of our faith, who for the joy that lay before Him endured a cross and despised the shame and has sat down at the right hand of God's throne."
HEBREWS 12:1–2

Up to this point in my journey, I've experienced periods of deafening darkness, moments of flickering light, and seasons where my heart is overwhelmed with joy amidst the hard. I am not naïve to think my family and I won't experience more difficult things. However, what the Lord has impressed upon my heart over these last few years as I've lived with an imperfect heart will anchor my soul when the fears come creeping back into my thoughts and the next season of suffering roars its ugly head. I will need to be reminded of God's promises and of His Truth when the next season of hard comes. I'm guessing that you will need to be reminded, too.

Each twist and turn our lives take and every single circumstance that befalls us allows us the opportunity to trust in our unchanging God. Our God is trustworthy. Our God is faithful. Our God is always present. Our God is in control. Our God is steadfast. Our God is our Rock and our Fortress and our Salvation. God remains God in the good and the bad, in the rejoicing and the devastation.

> *In the times when we feel near and in the times when we feel numb, God remains God.*

In the times when we feel near and in the times when we feel numb, God remains God. He is the same yesterday, today, and tomorrow. From our darkest days to our most glorious days, God stays the same. He is perfect. He is loving. He is powerful. He is holy. His loving pursuit of each one of our souls is unceasing. Feel free to remind me of this.

I need Jesus. Whether I have a heart requiring medication to support its function or a perfectly healthy, athletic heart, I need Him. Whether John goes to see the Lord in heaven before me, or we celebrate sixty years of marriage together, I need Jesus. Whether my boys outlive me here on this earth or I outlive them, I need Jesus. No measure of self-sufficiency or self-reliance will lessen the daily need for the Lord in my life. Before my diagnosis I found my identity in how productive I could be. I prided myself in how much knowledge I could acquire. And I thrived on competition whether athletic, academic, or professional. In hindsight, I had clearly compartmentalized the living God. Not with overt intentionality. Rather, I had gained too much confidence that I could handle most things in my life without needing Jesus. Oh, how wrong I was! I need our unchanging God every day, every breath, every heartbeat.

The way I view this life has shifted. The lens through which I view suffering has changed. The lens through which I view everyday, routine life has changed. I believe my life is not about *me*. Rather my life is a vessel for our God to use—and use wherever and however He deems best.

You know what else? Your life is not all about you. The days we are given are offered to us by the Creator of life. He is the one who tells the waves where to stop, and He is the One that breathes air into our lungs. My life, your life, was created to honor, praise, and live for our unchanging God. Nothing more. Nothing less. All things were created by God and for God. So, yes, this life is not my own.

This shift in perspective has caused me to look for the eternal in the small and big moments of my days. I no longer view my children as really cute mini-me's but souls for discipleship. I do not just want to play with them and read books to them in order to generate joy on their faces. I want to play with them so they might know the love of Jesus. I do not want to parent in a way that makes *my* life easier. I want to parent in the way that is inconvenient to me with the hope that my boys will grow in character and not entitlement. I want to spend ten extra minutes visiting with patients and their families behind clinic doors or hospital room curtains so they feel valued and cared for. I want them to know that I see beyond the diagnosis and see them as someone's son, daughter, sister, or brother. I want my life to be centered on my God, not God centered on me. After all, He is the giver of life, and He has given me life here on Earth and for eternity with Him in heaven. My hope is that you, too, will begin to see a perspective shift in your own life.

The Lord has given each one of us a race to run. Our races will not all look the same. Some will run on smooth ground as if circling a high school track, while others are crossing treacherous crevices in the most remote parts of the world. No race is greater. No race is less or more significant. God has specifically tailored each of our races purposefully for His pursuit of our affections and our worship.

God has specifically tailored each of our races purposefully for His pursuit of our affections and our worship.

Hebrews 12:1–2 implores us to run our race with endurance and with our eyes fixed on the prize of the hope of glory to be received through Jesus Christ. Yes, our race in this life will likely include differing portions of downhill where the running is easy. During these times, please do not be fooled to think you can run on your own strength. For just up ahead there will be mountainous climbs and there will be deep, dark valleys. There will be moments when you will struggle to catch your breath as you climb up steep terrain. May I suggest pausing to lift your eyes during these moments and look out at the beauty of the mountains surrounding you even though you have so much more to climb? My prayer is that as each one of us continues on, pushing forward in our race no matter what circumstance comes to pass, our hearts will continue on in desperation for Jesus. May we press forward with passion, knowing that God's purpose and His plan for our sanctification are perfect even in our suffering.

You've seen the wrestling of my own heart through these pages. I know we won't live this out perfectly. I know there will be many times in our life when we find ourselves reactively responding to the

May we press forward with passion, knowing that God's purpose and His plan for our sanctification are perfect even in our suffering.

fallout of our circumstances. We may even rely on our own logical wisdom, strength, knowledge, and deflective humor to maneuver through our sufferings. However, I'm so thankful to have another way to live. A way that causes me to lean into Jesus in the midst of both the good and the hard. We cannot and should not go through this life without relying on Him.

The Lord has been so gracious to me. He has given me seven years with my boys postdiagnosis—more days than I ever anticipated. I treasure being the wife to my beloved husband. I cherish each hug, high-five, and conversation I have with my three boys. Hunter will be in first grade when this book makes it into your hands. Noah will be in third grade, and Joshua will be two years old. Even though the Lord has multiplied my days, I am even more grateful Jesus continues to grow my affections for Him despite the unknowns. I will not take today for granted. I will live for Christ in the remaining moments I am given here on earth, even if my time is filled with suffering. My heart will persevere the hard and the valleys because of the hope I have in Christ.

When our eyes are focused on the eternal and not on the fleeting, we find hope that is unaffected by our circumstances. Unshakable hope is found in Jesus. The eternal hope says that one day all things will be made new, and there will be a day when our faith becomes sight. My hope does not lie in the present. My hope is placed in one day being home. With my eyes set on heaven, I must trust and believe that the Lord will endure me through today's and tomorrow's circumstances. This earth is not our home. I know where home is. Heaven is our prize. Beholding the glory of God is our prize. And the prize given to us is worth more than anything this life could throw at us.

I want to finish my race with focused eyes and a full heart. Is this your desire, too? What is the story Jesus is writing over your own life and your own soul? Would life look different if you held the perspective that your every breath and heartbeat rests in His hands? Because it does. What keeps your hope securely placed in the unseen, that which is to come? Of this I am certain, one day our faith *will* become sight. So come on! Let's lace up our running shoes. We've got a race set before us.

I'll see you at the finish line.

Boys,

You have a race to run. I cannot tell you what obstacles you will face as you run, but I can tell you that we have a God

BIG enough to strengthen you, persevere you and endure you through the racecourse every single footfall. God is God, and He never changes. May His Word continually be in your thoughts and on your lips. May Jesus use your lives of purpose to bring glory to Himself, and may you live a life of hope in and continual surrender to our unchanging God.

I love you to heaven and back . . . and back again.

I'll see you at home!

my heart, mommy

Notes

1. Wayne Grudem, *Bible Doctrine: Essential Teachings of the Christian Faith* (Grand Rapids, MI: Zondervan, 1999), 98.

2. Definition found in KeyWord Bible, NASB.

3. Edward Mote, "My Hope Is Built."